CATCH THE VISION

*The Life of
Henry L. Whitfield
of Mississippi*

BILL R. BAKER

UNIVERSITY PRESS OF MISSISSIPPI
JACKSON

Copyright © 1974 by the
University Press of Mississippi
Library of Congress Catalog Card Number 74-82918
ISBN 0-87805-062-0
Manufactured in the United States of America
Printed by Benson Printing Company, Nashville, Tennessee
Designed by Barney McKee

Contents

Preface vii

Foreword ix

1 State Superintendent of Education 3

2 President, Mississippi Industrial Institute and College 40

3 Governor of Mississippi 78

4 Legislative Program of the Whitfield Administration 116

Appendix: Genealogy of Henry Lewis Whitfield 153

Bibliography 155

Index 171

Preface

Henry L. Whitfield has been a forgotten figure in Mississippi history for almost fifty years. I am most grateful for the privilege of reconstructing and reassessing the life of this illustrious Mississippian. Following a successful tenure as schoolteacher and administrator at Steen's Creek, Mississippi, he became State Superintendent of Education. In this position he traveled throughout Mississippi urging the people to give greater emphasis to education. In the wake of his zealous activity came the rise of agricultural high schools, greater emphasis on vocational high schools, acceptance of physical education into the school system, and a new impetus for teacher training.

In 1907 Whitfield became President of Mississippi Industrial Institute and College, where he inspired many improvements and saw the number in the graduating class climb from 23 to 129. In 1923 he faced Theodore G. Bilbo in a hard campaign for Governor of Mississippi. His victory brought a new era in state politics. As Governor of Mississippi he was responsible for creating a new image of integrity for the state, placing the state on a solid financial foundation, opening the door to outside capital and industry, establishing the State Forestry Commission, and beginning the Mississippi State Hospital at Whitfield.

The completion of this biography has caused me to sense a feeling of gratitude to many people. Every name could not be mentioned. However, I must include the following: Dr. John K. Bettersworth, Academic Vice President of Mississippi State University, who suggested the idea; Dr. R. A. McLemore, retired director of the Mississippi Archives and History Department, who wrote the foreword; the Mississippi State University Department of History; members of the Whitfield family, who eagerly assisted me; Henry M. Whitfield, who made available the Robert Allen Whitfield papers; Mrs. Harry Artz Alexander, who provided invaluable information on the family background of H. L. Whitfield; the staff of Mitchell Memorial Library, Mississippi State University; the staff of the Mississippi Archives and History Department; the staff of the John Clayton Fant Memorial Library, Mississippi University for Women; the staff of the Mississippi College Library, Clinton; approximately 350 Mississippi Industrial Institute and College Alumnae who attended the college under Whitfield and either granted interviews to me or responded by mail to my plea for help—words could never describe the gracious disposition of these ladies; the fourteen living members of the 1924 legislature who granted interviews; many others who responded to my letters and granted interviews; the Mississippi Education Association for providing old copies of the *Mississippi Educational Advance;* Mrs. R. B. Lampton, who gave me her father's scrapbook of the 1923 Governor's campaign and one of Whitfield's campaign posters; Miss Marcie Sanders, who shared material with me from the files of the Mississippi University for Women Alumnae Office; Mrs. Mary Frances Ford for copying sections from her father's memoirs for me; Mississippi University for Women for permission to use the unpublished history of the university by Miss Sarah Neilson; Mrs. Mary Massey Whitworth for allowing me to use her scrapbook; Jill, my lovely wife, for her patience, sacrifice and encouragement during five years of researching and writing this book; Henry L. Whitfield, the inspiration from whose life helped me "catch the vision!"

B. R. B.

Clinton, Mississippi
August, 1974

Foreword

Catch the Vision—The Life of Henry L. Whitfield of Mississippi is a sympathetic account of one of Mississippi's most versatile and distinguished citizens. In the preparation of this work, Bill R. Baker has searched archives and libraries for relevant materials. He has conducted oral interviews or corresponded with more than 350 individuals whose personal involvement or knowledge of the events of the period furnished information for the biographical story. The exhaustive research gave Baker a voluminous store of information on which to base his account.

In the beginning, the author gives a brief overview of Whitfield's ancestry, tells the story of his boyhood, his early education, and his work as State Superintendent of Education. Baker found in Whitfield's boyhood and in his early professional experience many of the forces that proved to be guiding lights for him throughout his career. Whitfield's vision of the great potential for development in Mississippi and his belief that education was the key to unlock the store of riches is made manifest in this chapter. The stage on which Whitfield operated was vastly expanded when he was invited by Governor A. J. McLaurin in 1898 to serve an unexpired term as State Superintendent of Education. He was one of the youngest men to serve in this important post. Baker reveals in this account of his services the successes Whitfield achieved in preaching the theme, "Catch the Vision."

Whitfield's successful administration of the public school system led to his nomination as President of Mississippi Industrial Institute and College. During his thirteen-year tenure as President of the institution, Whitfield continued to be an earnest and successful advocate of his theories of education. He was particularly concerned that practical education be emphasized. The President succeeded in increasing the enrollment of the institution, in increasing support funds, in developing the physical plant, and in raising academic standards. Under his administration, the college gained admission to the Southern Association of Colleges and Schools, in recognition of the high quality of its work. Baker reveals in his study that one of the great resources Whitfield commanded was the affection and support of the students and faculty.

Whitfield was not a neophyte in the political world, but his announcement of his candidacy for the governorship caught some of his friends by surprise. In a turbulent political campaign in which former Governor Theodore G. Bilbo was his principal opponent, Whitfield proved adequate to the challenge. He commanded the support of the anti-Bilbo and the anti-Vardaman factions. One of his greatest assets was the support of the newly enfranchised women of Mississippi, led by former students of the Industrial Institute and College. Baker notes the old factional lines were still evident, but Whitfield was successful in breaking the solidarity of the Bilbo-Vardaman faction and won by a majority of approximately 16,000 votes.

In his study, Baker reveals that Whitfield's far-ranging interests were evident in his broad legislative program. He commanded the support of important leaders in the Senate and the House of Representatives. With this assistance, he was successful in persuading the legislature to adopt one of the most constructive programs that had been approved by any legislature. The measure of his success is the fact that this administration is generally regarded as a turning point in the history of the state.

This very complete and thorough account of Henry Lewis Whitfield suggests that the state's historical literature might be enriched by the preparation of biographical accounts of other chief executives. Baker has opened up new vistas for the historian in this excellent biography.

R. A. McLemore

CATCH THE VISION

1 · State Superintendent of Education

A special train, composed of several coaches and two private cars, left Jackson, Mississippi, on 19 March 1927. Among the passengers on the train, which was bound for Columbus, were members of the Governor's staff, a detail from the 155th Infantry of Jackson, newspaper reporters, a Baptist pastor, and dignitaries of the state—all in mourning! When the train pulled into Canton all the business houses were closed and thousands of people with bowed heads gathered at the depot.[1]

Near one of the railroad crossings a group of Boy Scouts stood at attention and saluted as the train passed by. Negroes, working on a central Mississippi farm, paused from their work and stood reverently with bowed heads when they spotted the train. A little boy was playing in his yard near Pheba when the billowing black smoke and the noise of the steam locomotive announced the approach of the train. He was confused because a train had never been seen on the track at that hour and he knew the schedule of all the trains. He was further confounded when he saw white flags waving from the engine and black drapes on one of the cars. This was a new sight and the curiosity of the small lad had to be satisfied. At that time a neighbor came along and told the boy that Henry L. Whitfield, Governor of Mississippi, had died and the train was carrying his body to Columbus for burial.

The train arrived at the Columbus depot late in the afternoon. Automobiles were lined up for miles and throngs of mourners

---

[1] Jackson *Daily News*, 19 March 1927; 20 March 1927.

4 CATCH THE VISION

waited. Leading the funeral procession were 1,200 uniformed girls from Mississippi State College for Women. The entire funeral party was over one mile in length.[2] According to the Governor's request, his body was buried in the old Friendship Cemetery near the banks of the Tombigbee River. From a humble beginning Henry Whitfield's vision had carried him from country schoolteacher to the Governor's Mansion by way of being the State Superintendent of Education and President of Mississippi State College for Women. His motto was "catch the vision;" self-improvement, state improvement, and service were the key concepts in his vision.

Born near Brandon, Mississippi, on 20 June 1868, Henry Lewis Whitfield descended from two of the largest and best-known families in the South, the Whitfields of North Carolina and the Fitzhughs of Virginia.[3] In 1837 Henry's grandfather, George William Whitfield, moved with his family from Johnston County, North Carolina, to Gainesville, Alabama, where he secured a home and plantation. About seventy-five slaves, including babies, were taken to the plantation and a white man was employed as overseer. George William and his wife were active members of the Gainesville Baptist Church and practiced their Christian faith in daily life. He would sometimes go out to his plantation and preach the Gospel to his Negroes.[4]

Following the death of George William Whitfield in 1842, General Nathan B. Whitfield of Demopolis, Alabama, moved the six children to his home and became their guardian and administrator of the estate. Included among the six children was four-year-old Robert Allen Whitfield, the father of Henry Lewis Whitfield. Robert was not overjoyed with his new surroundings because of deafness, which made him unpopular and unattractive to other children, and the skeptical attitude which his uncle demonstrated toward religion.[5]

---

[2] Ibid.
[3] Dunbar Rowland, *The Official and Statistical Register of the State of Mississippi 1924–1928* (New York, 1928), p. 58.
[4] "Memoirs of Robert Allen Whitfield" 1:6–7 in possession of Henry M. Whitfield, Tupelo, Miss.
[5] Ibid., pp. 8–10.

In 1854 Robert was sent to Harrisburg, Pennsylvania, to a school for the deaf. He later studied for a short time at the University of North Carolina and the University of Virginia. Although he continued to remain a good student, this was the extent of his formal education.[6]

In 1859 Robert visited his brother, who lived near Brandon. He immediately fell in love with Rankin County, bought a small place there, and settled down to begin a bachelor's life. The bachelor's life came to an abrupt end in 1860 when he married Mollie Fitzhugh, a beautiful girl with exceptional talent for singing and playing the piano. He went to teach in the Fannin school, located approximately eleven miles north of Brandon, and remained there for fifteen years.[7]

Robert Allen Whitfield remained a deeply religious person and in every good fortune gave the credit to Jesus Christ, whom he took for a friend in his youth. He wanted his children to understand that the reason he received four large schools was the goodness of God, who directed and helped him. In his teaching he emphasized the spiritual development of the pupils. His religious verve led him to be ordained a Baptist minister while teaching at Fannin, an action that was neither requested nor resisted by Robert.[8]

At the time Henry Lewis Whitfield was born, the Civil War was causing untold hardships. His father was broken financially by the war but was able to retain a small farm of eighty acres. While the father taught school, young Henry and his brother, Robert, farmed. Mrs. Whitfield gave music lessons to the young ladies of the area in order to add to the family income.

Henry attended school in Fannin and ultimately took a teacher's examination that qualified him for a license to teach school. Beginning his teaching career at the age of seventeen, he succeeded his father as teacher in both the Oak Grove and the Westville schools in Simpson County.[9]

---

[6] Ibid., pp. 26, 38.
[7] Ibid., pp. 45, 56.
[8] Ibid., pp. 61–62, 79–80.
[9] R. A. McLemore and Nannie Pitts McLemore, *Mississippi Through Four Centuries* (Chicago, 1945), p. 294; "Memoirs of R. A. Whitfield" 1:79.

COURTESY BILLY WHITFIELD

Henry Whitfield at fourteen years of age

Henry Whitfield continued to teach school, save money, and pursue his studies at Mississippi College, a Baptist school located in Clinton.[10] During his years on the campus of this college, he exhibited the same commendable attributes that later characterized his life. He wanted to serve his fellowman rather than himself and never to escape responsibility. He responded energetically to every commission assigned to him whether in the classroom or on the campus. He had a reputation for trustworthiness, responsibility, and commendable character.[11]

During the student days at Mississippi College Whitfield was very active in the literary societies and supported them en-

[10] Jackson *Daily News*, 6 December 1925.
[11] Ibid., 20 January 1924.

thusiastically. He was known to love good books and was a familiar sight in the college library where he devoted much time to browsing.[12] As a college student he became well known for his oratorical ability, winning the Trotter Medal for oratory over a number of competitors in his junior year. This same year he was also the speaker for the Philomathean Society.[13]

Kind and considerate of others, Whitfield was very popular and appreciated by the students at Mississippi College. On one occasion when a student was harshly reprimanded by the professor for having come to the class poorly prepared, Whitfield visited the student every night for the remainder of the semester in order to assist him with the difficult studies. The student later became a prominent businessman in a neighboring state, and he, along with the faculty and students at Mississippi College, was never surprised with the success of Henry Whitfield. He was considered a success as a student and other successes would naturally follow.[14]

Leaving the Westville school, Whitfield became principal of the school at Steen's Creek (Florence), Mississippi, a boarding school and the only high school in the county. It attracted students from as far away as Yazoo City. "Professor" was the title given the new mentor of the Steen's Creek school. The students loved him even though he was very strict as a disciplinarian and expected them to abide by exact rules and regulations. Whitfield was respected and looked upon as a good teacher.

When Professor Whitfield came to Steen's Creek he had only one assistant and approximately sixty students. Later a second assistant was added, and the student body grew to over one hundred. A music room was added to the school building to encourage the students in the fine arts.

The entire community of Steen's Creek loved and appreciated Henry Whitfield, and they considered themselves very fortunate to have a man of such calibre to direct the school. Throughout

[12] Ibid.; Editorial, *The Mississippi Educational Advance* 10(1919):10.
[13] Jackson *Daily News*, 20 January 1924; Editorial, *The Mississippi Educational Advance* 10(1919):10.
[14] Jackson *Daily News*, 20 January 1924.

8 CATCH THE VISION

Faculty and student body at Steens Creek School in 1896—Henry Whitfield is seated on front row

his tenure there his popularity with the townspeople never waned. A favorite story in Steen's Creek was that one night Professor Whitfield was awakened by a bizarre pandemonium. Running out into the open middle hall he discovered that fox hounds had chased a fox right through the hall. One of his former students remarked that he never heard anything bad about the professor. In Whitfield's classes students were often called upon to stand and recite answers to his questions.

While teaching at Steen's Creek Henry Whitfield married Mary Dampeer White, the petite, attractive daughter of Dr. William White. Dr. White was a member of the state board of health for many years and one of the best-known physicians in the state of Mississippi. Henry and Mary had four sons: Robert Allen, Knox White, Henry Lewis, Jr., and William White.[15]

The religious character and interest of Henry Whitfield was very obvious to the students at Steen's Creek school, inasmuch as he wanted them to develop in spirit as well as in mind and body. An active participant in church affairs, he welcomed the

---

[15] Dunbar Rowland, *History of Mississippi: The Heart of the South*, 4 vols. (Jackson 1925) 3:5. Knox and Henry, Jr. are deceased; Robert and William live in Columbus, Miss.

opportunity to preach in churches although he was never ordained as a minister. A familiar sight in the pulpit of the Steen's Creek Baptist Church, he was considered an excellent preacher by members of the congregation. He eagerly accepted invitations for all kinds of speaking engagements. He simply enjoyed making speeches and people were delighted to listen.

Henry Whitfield was obsessed with the idea of educating people and wanted to enrich the minds of all he could possibly reach. Convinced that a trained mind was the key to the better life, he helped many people receive an education, including a brother who probably would not have received an education had it not been for Henry. Professor Whitfield brought his brother to Steen's Creek and kept him in his home to enable him to attend the school. This brother later received his degree in medicine and became the Director of the Bureau of Vital Statistics in Mississippi.

Whitfield's college career was different from many because he never attended college two years in succession. Interspersing his college career with teaching, he was finally graduated from Mississippi College in 1895, ten years after first enrolling. Later he did some study at the University of Mississippi.[16] The vision that he had for himself was never dimmed by the difficulty of the tasks, and he constantly strived for excellence in personal achievement.

Throughout all the years of formal study, Whitfield's ambition had been to become a lawyer. With this goal in mind he enrolled and completed a course in law at Millsaps College in Jackson. In 1898 he was on the verge of entering law practice when an unexpected turn of events greatly altered his life. At that time State Superintendent of Education A. A. Kincannon was elected President of the Industrial Institute and College in Columbus. Governor A. J. McLaurin called upon Whitfield to fill Kincannon's unexpired term. There were other men in contention for the appointment, but Whitfield had an advantage with his reputation as an excellent schoolteacher that had been

---

[16] Rowland, *History of Mississippi* 3:5.

established at Steen's Creek, and he and the Governor were personal friends from the same county.[17] He served out the unexpired term and was elected for two full terms with no opposition.

Henry Whitfield came to the office of Mississippi State Superintendent of Education possessing great faith in the future of the state. He understood that the South had just passed through a time of unparalleled agony and distress. Property had been destroyed, the social system swept away, and a great number of the state's outstanding young men slain on the battlefields. He had witnessed the South giving her first attention to those objects necessary for physical survival. Convinced that the hour of darkness and hopelessness was passing and envisioning a new climate of courage and self-reliance, he challenged the people to rebuild wisely.[18]

The youthful state leader had a philosophy of education that the state of Mississippi desperately needed at the turn of the century. At this time an abundance of attention was given to the material resources of the state, but Whitfield helped the citizens to understand that material resources alone do not make a state great. He taught that trained minds were essential in the wise use of natural resources. His argument was based on the fact that many people in the world lived in close proximity to nature's bountiful gifts while contributing absolutely nothing to the advance of civilization. To illustrate he cited Mexico with her mineral wealth, good climate, and rich soil, which ranked zero in the world's estimation. He also claimed the same for the South and Central American countries.[19]

Whitfield cited Switzerland and Holland as examples of places with poor soil and imperfect climates that had given much to the world, and the people were blessed and happy. He was satisfied that in any country the people could become happy and

---

[17] E. H. Ratcliff to Governor McLaurin, 8 August 1898; D. M. Huff to Governor McLaurin, 12 August 1898, A. J. McLaurin Collection, Series E, Mississippi State Department of Archives, Jackson, Miss.
[18] Jackson *Daily Clarion-Ledger*, 19 January 1903.
[19] Ibid.

prosperous if they were equipped with proper education and training. The new State Superintendent of Education preached that an illiterate citizenry could live among the preferred gratuities of heaven while making no advance. On the other hand, he argued that a well-trained people will soar above the most inauspicious surroundings and make their mark among the accomplishments of the world.[20] The people of Mississippi were to hear him say repeatedly, "There is more in the man than in the land." [21]

The State Superintendent of Education proclaimed that lack of training and slothfulness had prevented the people of Mississippi from becoming personally involved in developing the natural resources. He was alarmed that so much of the land in the state had been purchased by nonresidents, and that so much skilled labor had come from outside the state while the local residents were doing the ordinary jobs and receiving low wages. He believed that if the people were not trained they would simply become onlookers to the development of the state's natural resources. He conceded that the Reconstruction period had crushed the people in many ways, yet he thought there could be a brighter day if they could only catch the vision of training the children for the opportunities. Since people can do only what they are trained to do, Whitfield insisted that the training of Mississippians should receive precedence over everything. People of the state heard their educational leader fervently declare that the success of the schools would determine the future successes in the state.[22]

Superintendent Whitfield affirmed that the state could be developed only in direct proportion to the development of the people. He viewed the people as the great producing cause and diligently attended the cause, believing the effects would take care of themselves. "All our institutions, material developments,

[20] Ibid.
[21] Henry L. Whitfield, *Speech, On the Subject of "State Finances"* (Jackson, 1924), p. 32.
[22] Henry L. Whitfield, "An Address by State Superintendent H. L. Whitfield," *Proceedings of the Mississippi Teachers Association* (May 1905), pp. 134–35.

and the character of work we are doing," he claimed, "are but barometers indicating the real condition of the people." [23]

The educational philosophy of Whitfield was that of a warrior in battle, with ignorance the enemy. To him the enemy was like a malignancy contaminating and destroying everything it touched. This enemy stood in the path of all progress, hampered all great inventions, prevented the writing of great books and the painting of notable works of art, and was the breeder of crime and the spawner of superstition.[24]

The philosophy of education expounded by Whitfield encompassed far more than the knowledge gained from a textbook, which, to him, was never to be considered an end itself. Never willing to separate the development of the mind from moral and ethical development, he wanted Mississippi schools to foster young men and women of high ideals, too strong to do anything base or sordid. Anxious to develop young people who were not only strong in mind but also strong in determination to stand against all wrong, Whitfield wanted more than exemplary minds —he wanted exemplary lives.[25]

On the premise that the estimate of a person's life is determined by his actions, Whitfield went beyond the acts to teach that thoughts determine actions, and thoughts, in turn, are based on the knowledge which a person possesses. Therefore, he viewed the mind as the fountain of life which must be kept pure in order that only virtuous influences might emanate from it. His philosophy emphasized that proper education should help the student cultivate a taste for that which is high and good, while at the same time creating an antagonism for that which is virulent and pernicious.[26]

One of the significant themes in the educational philosophy of Henry Whitfield was his emphasis on work, and his personal accomplishments served as sufficient testimony to the reward of

---

[23] H. L. Whitfield, "A Greater Mississippi," *Four Masterpieces on Education, Unionism and Labor Problems,* ed. W. W. Welch (Jackson, n.d.), pp. 31-32.
[24] Jackson *Daily Clarion-Ledger,* 19 January 1903.
[25] Ibid.
[26] Ibid.

industry. He was ordinarily a patient man, but he was impatient with those who were afraid of work, and he taught that no one had the right to receive something for nothing if he were able to work. The school was viewed as moving toward an untenable position when emphasis was not properly given to work and industry.[27]

The teachers of the state were encouraged by Whitfield to educate the "brains and the hands" of the people.[28] This concept resulted in a close relationship and friendship with Professor Lawrence C. Jones, founder of the Piney Woods School. Jones and Whitfield often talked together about their concept of education—education of the head, heart, and hands. Professor Jones said they agreed on the importance of book knowledge, but they also agreed that total education of a person included more than formal schooling. When visiting Piney Woods School, Whitfield encouraged the students to take advantage of every opportunity and go as far as their ability would carry them.

The Whitfield philosophy of education could not be separated from the ideals of the Christian faith. He was a religious person who was emphatic in his conviction that religion should be taught in the schools. Desiring honesty in religion rather than a creed, he emphasized the necessity of a person's religious creed conforming to his conduct and conversation. Viewing the Bible as the greatest of all books and considering it necessary for self-control and fulfillment of purpose, he could not conceive of a school where there was no reading of the Holy Scriptures.

When Whitfield became State Superintendent of Education, the South was experiencing an educational rebirth. Personalities such as J. L. M. Curry and forces exemplified by the General Educational Board were obvious factors in this renaissance. The new Superintendent of Education was in contact with all of the ideas and work of such leaders and forces.[29] In order to place

---

[27] Henry L. Whitfield, "The Field of Activity for the Normal College," *The Mississippi Educational Advance* 1(1911):7.
[28] Whitfield, "A Greater Mississippi," p. 36.
[29] Anne L. Fant, "Henry Lewis Whitfield, Educator, Governor, Christian Gentleman," *The Mississippi Educational Advance* 18(1927):313.

him in the mainstream of American life, and Southern life in particular, emphasis must be given to the forces at work in the area of education. Since Whitfield was a well-informed person, he could not be separated from certain personalities and developments on the educational scene.

The modification of the school programs in order to create a new day in the South was expounded by John E. Seaman, a New Orleans schoolman, in 1885. In an address entitled "High Schools and the State," he spoke of the connection between the high school and the increasing demands of the new industrial life. He said that more young people would be attending high school if the schools could adjust to the pressing needs of the day.[30] Therefore, at the turn of the century, industrial and educational development became the two-pronged fork to lift the South out of defeat and dismay.

Between 1876 and 1900 the South had made little progress in the field of public education. The economic situation in the South was not conducive to the growth of public education. The schools desperately needed money and there were few funds available. Material resources had been depleted by the war, and, during the twenty-five years following the war, material development advanced at a snail's pace. The treasuries of the states were exhausted, and the one-crop economy of the South saw each crop made by a mortgage on itself. Economic depression hung like a heavy cloud over the South. Southerners were poor but had not realized that their poverty resulted largely from poor schools.[31]

Prior to 1910 antipathy hampered the growth of public education. Public officials had made promises regarding the schools which were not kept, and the unqualified local school officers had destroyed the confidence of the citizens. Because of this attitude, there developed a disposition of lukewarmness and even antagonism toward the schools. The South had been engaged

---

[30] R. Freeman Butts and Lawrence A. Cremin, *A History of Education in American Culture* (New York, 1953), p. 366.
[31] Edgar W. Knight, *Public Education in the South* (Boston, 1922), pp. 416–17.

State Superintendent of Education 15

in a battle for political endurance that compelled education to assume a stance that was almost calamitous.[32]

Education in the South was plagued by perverted politics. Nearly every aspect of education came under the unwholesome influence of unprincipled public officials and political bosses who misused the schools in the pursuit of personal profit. The so-called "courthouse ring," a dominant influence in most Southern towns, generally placed the well-being of the school below its political ambitions. In many instances the positions in public education were considered political plums for the victors rather than opportunities for qualified persons to become servants of the public.[33]

Many conservative and aristocratic citizens were convinced that the provisions for education were sufficient. They believed that the state had no responsibility in the field of public education, but rather viewed the matter as a responsibility of the parents. They opposed the taxation of property for support of the public schools and generally embraced the theory of white supremacy.[34] These persons, "clinging to the conservative tradition, held that education should not be a function of the state anymore than provision for food and shelter." [35] Some of the conservatives, typified by the theologian Robert L. Dabney, opposed the leveling effect of public education. They disagreed with any educational approach where the children of the well-to-do would become companions of the lowly.[36] As a result, many of the poor people did not attend the schools because they were so inadequate.

Another impediment to the progress of public education was the matter of race. The Negro had been the center of interest during the period of Reconstruction. Through no fault of their own, many Negroes were used by scheming politicians in this period.

---

[32] Ibid., p. 418.
[33] Ibid., pp. 418–19.
[34] Ibid., p. 423.
[35] Francis B. Simkins, *A History of the South* (New York, 1963), p. 363.
[36] Ibid., pp. 362–63.

16 CATCH THE VISION

When one understands such concepts he will have greater appreciation for the problems which faced Whitfield and recognize the necessity for certain programs which he advocated.

All of these conditions resulted in an appalling situation for the South at the turn of the century. In 1900 the money provided for each school-age child in the South ranged from $.50 in Alabama and North Carolina to $1.46 in Florida and Texas. The average for the United States was $2.84. The average school term in the South was less than one hundred days, whereas the average for the United States was approximately one hundred and forty-five days. Salaries for the teachers were pathetically low. The average monthly salary for a schoolteacher was $24 in North Carolina and Alabama, $32 in Mississippi and Virginia, and $34 in Florida. In addition to low salaries, the payment of the salaries was often uncertain.[37]

There was no compulsory state school law in any Southern state before 1900. Only 10 percent of the pupils enrolled reached the fifth grade and only one pupil out of seventy progressed to the eighth grade. The illiteracy rate among the white population of the South was three times greater than the national average. One Negro out of two and one white man out of five could not read and write. "Outside the cities little attempt was made in the public schools to bridge the gap between the grammar grades and college." [38]

Many of the teachers taught only what they wanted to teach or whatever they felt qualified to teach and often with little thought for the needs of the pupils. Some of the teachers did as well as they were able, but too many of them did no more than keep the doors of the school open. The schools were inadequately graded and the teaching methods were uninspiring and unchallenging. The school administrators from the local to the state level frequently did not possess the training, superinten-

[37] Ibid., pp. 363, 420.
[38] Knight, *Public Education in the South*, p. 420; C. Vann Woodward, *Origins of the New South 1877–1913*, in *A History of the South* ed. Wendell Holmes Stephenson and E. Merton Coulter, 10 vols. (Baton Rouge, 1949–1967) 9:368; Simkins, *A History of the South*, p. 363.

dency, and other skills to function efficiently in their jobs. The County Superintendent usually held brief tenure and received a low salary. There were no exact qualifications for the office of County Superintendent, and, in some cases, it was not expected that he be educated. The position was often filled by incompetent persons who had succeeded in nothing else.[39]

The schoolhouses, especially in the rural area, were frequently no more than crude log structures or broken-down buildings, some not even equipped with windows, desks, tables, blackboards, maps, and other necessities. Some of the buildings were furnished with only rough benches with no backs. In 1900 the average value of a rural schoolhouse in the South was approximately $100.[40]

The organization and supervision of the school work left much to be desired. Most of the smaller schools were operated with no assistance from the state and county officials. In many cases the trustees of the school were only concerned with providing a job for some friend or relative. The results of this were that the number of schoolhouses increased as influential families selfishly satisfied their own interests, and there was no strict enforcement of teacher examination. These tragedies were augmented by the fact that 90 percent of the children looked to the rural schools for their education.[41]

Before the turn of the century conditions improved somewhat. There was a rebirth of the educational press which gave new impetus to school improvements. Teachers' institutes and teachers' reading-circle work assisted in awakening a sleeping educational potential.[42] However, the public schools before 1900 were in a pitiful state with spasmodic attendance and half-hearted and half-qualified teachers. The South lagged far behind the educational accomplishments of other sections of the country in almost all areas. In the opinion of one of the foremost scholars

[39] Knight, *Public Education in the South*, pp. 421–22.
[40] Ibid., p. 421.
[41] Ibid., p. 422.
[42] Ibid., p. 424.

of the New South, "Southern education suffered from a greater lag than any other public institution in the region." [43]

One should deal fairly with the South and point out certain problems in the field of education that placed her in a peculiar category when compared with the remainder of the country. For example, there was a greater proportion of children to adults which made the situation more acute. In New York there were 125 adult males to every 100 children of school age, whereas there were 66 adult males to every 100 children of school age in Mississippi. The typical adult in Mississippi had approximately twice as many children to educate as the adults living in the Northern states, and the burden was made even heavier because there was less money with which to accomplish this task.[44]

Around the turn of the century several things were happening to bring about a new direction in Southern education. All of these were to have their influence on Henry Whitfield and Mississippi. First, the New South began to take definite steps toward a new economic growth. Obviously no adequate system of education could be possible without a corresponding economic advance. At this time there was an increase in cotton production, new industries appeared on the scene, sizable capital was channeled into cotton manufacturing, and new railroads were built throughout the South. From 1890 to 1900 there was a 50 percent increase in the wealth of the South. This brought in additional revenues for school support and helped change the attitude of many toward education in the South.[45]

Accompanying the increase in economic wealth was the rise of a dominant and persuasive middle class that was anxious to participate in the public affairs of the South. Late in the nineteenth century there was an awakened democracy accompanied by an upward movement among the middle class. As members of this class became more powerful they sought increased involvement in social and political life. In particular, they

---

[43] Woodward, *Origins of the New South*, p. 393.
[44] Ibid., p. 399.
[45] Knight, *Public Education in the South*, pp. 424-25.

positioned themselves on the cutting edge of educational development and insisted that the citizens be served by the schools.[46]

A third change that spurred the educational advance of the South around the turn of the century was the political alterations that took place. Several small political parties appeared on the scene such as the Union Labor party in Arkansas and the Young Men's Democracy in Louisiana, and these new parties advocated certain improvements in the realm of education. The strongest political movement was the Populist party, which developed strength throughout most of the South. This party became a significant influence for education, and even though the strength of the party declined by 1900, the influence continued. It became the "in" thing for political parties to call for new educational advantages around 1900.[47] The Farmer's Alliance should be cited for putting in motion certain educational influences that continued at the turn of the century. The Alliance was involved primarily in political purposes, but emphasis was also given to education.[48]

For twenty years following Reconstruction the race issue had impeded the interests of education. The situation became reversed when the race issue began to serve as a strong motivating force in education. When the constitutions of Southern states began to be amended to make literacy a requirement for voting, a requirement made applicable to both races, the thought of disfranchising illiterates changed the outlook tremendously. The value of education soared to new heights, and expanded educational facilities were demanded in order that all people might become informed and involved citizens.[49]

Another important development around the turn of the century that was destined to have far-reaching effects on Southern education was the appearance of a new breed of Southern leaders who had a vision of the future. Convinced that the South was

---

[46] Ibid., pp. 425–26.
[47] Ibid., pp. 426–27.
[48] Simkins, *A History of the South*, p. 350.
[49] Knight, *Public Education in the South*, p. 427.

overcoming the heartaches, financial limitations, and the political predicament resulting from the war, they also realized that the future of the South depended upon an educated populace.[50] "They were not men of millions, and for the most part they kept their skirts clear of politics. They were middle-class, professional people—schoolmen, churchmen, editors—inspired with humanitarian zeal and a passion for uplift."[51] With these men and Whitfield, who was one of them, came the "return of a sense of belongingness to the Union, coupled with the spread of traditional American ideas concerning universal schooling."[52]

An extremely important development in Southern education was the birth of the Conference for Education in the South. One of the urgent needs at the turn of the century was for some organized approach to disseminating information throughout the South concerning the educational conditions and needs. There were those persons dedicated to education who believed such an approach would instigate a new concept in public education. In great measure this need was met by the Conference. This idea had its inception in 1898 when a group of men and women met in Capon Springs, West Virginia, for a Conference on Christian Education in the South. At the second meeting in 1899 the name was changed to Conference for Education in the South. Several succeeding meetings were held in various cities. In 1901 the Southern Education Board was organized for the purpose of expanding services. A year later the General Education Board was formed. The assistance given to the South by this organization cannot be overestimated.[53]

The principal work of the Board was to "conduct a campaign of education for free schools for all the people by supplying literature to the newspapers and periodical press, by participation in education meetings, and by general correspondence."[54] Since

---

[50] Ibid., p. 426.
[51] Woodward, *Origins of the New South*, p. 396.
[52] Butts and Cremin, *A History of Education*, p. 414.
[53] Knight, *Public Education in the South*, p. 429.
[54] Butts and Cremin, *A History of Education*, p. 414.

State Superintendent of Education 21

the Board was only engaged in a campaign to get information to the people, it did not grant financial assistance to any school or institution. Among the aims of the Board were "voluntary local taxation for better schools, compulsory education, longer school terms, consolidation of weak schools, and industrial and agricultural education." [55]

The campaigns directed by the Conference for Education in the South were implemented in North Carolina in 1902, Virginia in 1903, Georgia and Tennessee in 1904, South Carolina and Alabama in 1905, and Arkansas and Florida in 1908. The campaign came to Mississippi in 1905 during the middle of Whitfield's tenure as Superintendent. He kept abreast of these new and exciting developments and was greatly influenced by them.[56]

In every area of the South changes for the better could be cited. Between 1900 and 1910 the revenue for schools increased between 100 and 200 percent. The value of schoolhouses was significantly increased and there was a substantial rise in enrollment and attendance. The percentage of illiteracy decreased from 27 to 18, and the length of the school term grew from 96.7 days in 1900 to 121.7 days in 1910. There was a noticeable increase in teacher salaries by 1910, although they remained low by national standards. Departments of education were established in the reputable colleges and universities of the South and the number of state-supported normal schools increased. A new emphasis was also given to the training of school administrators and high-school principals.[57]

This new support for Southern education resulted in the development of more high schools, especially in the rural areas. The trend toward consolidation was initiated, resulting in the fusion of certain smaller schools into larger ones. The consolidation effort provided better teachers, better equipment, and more complete curricula. Accompanying this fervent revival movement in education was the founding of rural libraries, organiza-

---

[55] Woodward, *Origins of the New South*, p. 402.
[56] Knight, *Public Education in the South*, p. 432; Fant, "Henry Lewis Whitfield," p. 313.
[57] Knight, *Public Education in the South*, p. 432.

tion of parent-teachers' associations, emphasis on better qualified County Superintendents and helpful laws respecting compulsory attendance and child labor.[58]

The approach of Henry Whitfield to his responsibilities as State Superintendent of Education was distinctive. He became more of a "field" man than an "office" man, though no one could accuse him of neglecting the duties of the office routine. He traveled throughout Mississippi stumping for better schools and living conditions in the state. Not only the cities but the smallest communities in Mississippi occupied a place in his heart. The State Superintendent went into all sections of Mississippi, visiting the schools and gathering firsthand information about the existing condition.[59]

In the educational awakening of New England in the nineteenth century Horace Mann had surveyed the state of Massachusetts. Henry Whitfield did the same thing for Mississippi in the early twentieth century. He aroused the people from their lethargy and challenged them to see educational improvement as the state's imperative commission. Proclaiming that the road to progress could be paved only with education, he stressed that, in light of the prevailing poor conditions in the state, there was no alternative to an improved educational system. His personal dedication to the cause of education is unquestionable when one considers the hardships he endured to canvass the state in a period of poor roads and substandard living conditions.[60]

During the period 1900–1903, Whitfield visited every section of Mississippi, appearing personally before 75,000 people. In this way he carried his one-man campaign for better schools to every corner of the state. Although he was greatly concerned by 1905 because his efforts had not resulted in complete success in all sections of the state, he did not forsake his vision or lower his goals. He could never be satisfied until the people of Mississippi placed the school interests of the state above all other interests.

---

[58] Ibid., p. 433.
[59] *The Mississippi Educational Advance* 10(1919):103; Ann Caulfield Winston, *A Sampler By A Mississippi Schoolteacher* (New York, 1954), p. 103.
[60] Fant, "Henry Lewis Whitfield," p. 313.

He wanted Mississippians to "catch the vision" of education and see it as the first parental responsibility and the most important province of the state. Whitfield said, "I know that our proud people will be the hewers of wood and drawers of water for the rest of the world until our people regard education as essential and not incidental." [61]

With other leading educators in the United States, Whitfield was concerned about vocational inefficiency. He bemoaned the fact that so many young people had never really been brought into comprehensive contact with the principal occupation of the state. The lands were becoming less productive, outdated implements were used, and many were still strangers to such practices as farm drainage, fertilization, rotation, and diversification of crops. Whitfield wanted every rural school in Mississippi to have a field laboratory where the young people could be taught the best methods of farming and the advantages of farm life. His vision evidently anticipated the Smith-Hughes Act of 1917, which gave the government the authority to establish a national program of vocational education. His ideas also paralleled those of E. L. Thorndike of Columbia University, who "encouraged vocational tendencies by stressing skills rather than by assuming that a broad education in a few academic subjects was beneficial and pervasive." [62]

Whitfield envisioned the use of modern implements and methods in farming which would result in a 400 percent increase in farm products. His vision also reached out to include the advantages of breeding the best stock. Although the State Superintendent was not antagonistic toward the learned professions, he was highly critical of anyone who taught that more brilliance and aptitude were required for these than for agriculture and its accompanying areas of industry. He told the people to close their eyes and catch the vision of well-worked highways, developed

---

[61] *Biennial Report of the State Superintendent of Public Education* (1903), pp. 4, 16; (1905), p. 7; hereafter cited as *Biennial Report of Superintendent*.
[62] Fant, "Henry Lewis Whitfield," p. 313; Whitfield, "The Field of Activity," p. 7; Harvey Wish, *Society and Thought in Modern America*, 2 vols. (New York, 1952) 2:140.

lands resulting from cultivation, diversification, and fertilization, and labor-saving equipment in the fields.[63]

In addition to farming, Whitfield wanted emphasis given to other forms of industry. The day of diversified industries was envisioned when numerous kinds of raw materials would be developed into finished products within the state. The State Superintendent argued that it was foolish to ship raw materials out of the state in order to have them returned as finished products.[64]

As Whitfield traveled over the state he discovered the deplorable condition of many farm women. The government had given some emphasis to better farming methods, thus assisting the man of the house, but nothing had been introduced to aid the farm wife. Consequently, he called upon the schools to offer home economics.[65] Dr. H. M. Ivy, prominent Mississippi educator, says that Whitfield must be credited with the initial expansion of home economics studies in Mississippi schools.

Whitfield encouraged the training of Mississippi youth in such manner as to enable them to obtain the choice gains from their rural lives. He wanted to make farm life attractive and profitable, and magnetic in holding the youth. There was great concern because so many of the capable leaders of rural life had deserted the farms for the cities. This trend could be halted only by making rural life as alluring as city life. Convinced that a new day would dawn for rural life if proper emphasis were given in the educational area, Whitfield wanted the youth to receive instruction in how to build and maintain comfortable homes with a cultural atmosphere.[66]

The State Superintendent encouraged the teachers to assist the youth in rural areas in adopting better methods of agriculture. Even though most of the boys had been reared in or near cotton fields, they were not intimately acquainted with new scientific means of growing cotton. They also needed lessons in the marketing of cotton and its products. The young people used the

[63] Whitfield, "A Greater Mississippi," pp. 27–28.
[64] Ibid., pp. 28–29.
[65] Fant, "Henry Lewis Whitfield," p. 313.
[66] *Biennial Report of Superintendent* (1903), p. 14.

same methods and implements as their fathers, and Whitfield desired to lift their sights to better agricultural methods. In his travels throughout the state, he concluded that what was true of cotton was also true of stock, poultry, orchards, and everything grown on the farm. Consequently, he became a driving force for including the teaching of the elements of agriculture in the curriculum of the schools.[67]

In the area of vocational training Whitfield obviously concentrated on the cultivation and utilization of the staple cotton in Mississippi. Throughout his life he had observed the shipping of cotton outside the state to distant towns where it was spun and woven into finished products, thereby bringing great profit to those towns. The same thing was true with almost all the raw materials in the state. The people of Mississippi could refine the raw materials into finished products if they had the training, but there were few factories in the state. Whitfield called for a detailed study of the state's raw materials followed by the building of miniature plants at Mississippi Agricultural and Mechanical College where young men could be trained to work in and manage larger plants that would eventually be built in Mississippi.[68]

This vision of the miniature plant was successfully conveyed to the state legislature, and in 1900 an act was passed establishing a textile school in connection with the Agricultural and Mechanical College. The new law stated that the plant should be designed to educate the young men in the work of manufacturing textile fabrics and to equip them with a "practical as well as theoretical and scientific knowledge of the art of manufacturing textile fabrics, and especially those made from cotton, or cotton and wool combined including dyeing, designing and drawing." [69]

Henry Whitfield wanted to see the establishment of a system of agricultural high schools in Mississippi. These schools would be designed to take the work that had been sufficiently tested by the college or experiment stations and put it into pragmatic op-

---

[67] Ibid., p. 14.
[68] Ibid. (1889), p. 12.
[69] Mississippi *Laws* (1900), chap. 116.

eration. This development was especially needed because the farmer, more than any other person, required the application of the new scientific methods. The legislature responded to this appeal by passing a law establishing agricultural high schools in Mississippi in 1908.[70]

Convinced that the physical development of the youth had been neglected, Whitfield made this a vital part of his educational emphasis. His theory was that as life becomes more complicated, the human body becomes susceptible to additional maladies. He challenged the teachers to give attention to the muscles as well as the mind. There was the fear that the new multipurpose machinery would make the people soft, since they did not have to exert themselves physically in providing every convenience of home and farm. This was especially alarming because Whitfield saw an interdependent relationship between body and mind which, for man to develop ideally, required a concurrent cultivation of both.[71] This concept resulted in the acceptance of physical education into the school system of Mississippi.

Whitfield, never veering from his stand on physical fitness, placed the responsibility for developing acceptable physical habits on the teachers. In the realization of desirable health conditions, the State Superintendent embraced the notion that the schools should become involved in the extirpation of disease and the subjugation of epidemics. The importance of this matter was imprinted indelibly on the mind of Whitfield by the smallpox and yellow fever epidemics that greatly curtailed the regular school attendance during his first year in office.[72]

Religion always played a vital role in the educational program of Henry Whitfield. He believed in God as the creator of all men and that children had been blessed by their creator with a rich endowment. However, since these endowments were in a dormant stage, the youth could achieve maximum productivity

---

[70] *Biennial Report of Superintendent* (1905, p. 20; Mississippi *Laws* (1908), chap. 102.
[71] Jackson *Daily Clarion-Ledger*, 19 January 1903.
[72] Whitfield, "The Field of Activity," p. 6; *Biennial Report of Superintendent* (1899), p. 1.

in society only through dedicated training. He defined the common school as the agency "which takes children with their native endowments and their pre-school experience and attempts to grow [sic] them into men and women who can perform completely the functions of life in a Christian civilization." He wanted the pupils to understand that their talents came from God by creation, and that they had the privilege and obligation to develop them to the greatest possible degree. Failure to do this should be accounted the greatest of sins.[73]

Another obvious accentuation in Whitfield's educational program was patriotism. His patriotic spirit was never questioned, and he taught that Mississippians ought to love their state, dedicate themselves to its welfare, and take pride in the honor and privilege of developing all her potentialities.[74] In order to promote patriotism, the State Superintendent worked with the Board of Education to establish December 10 as "Mississippi Day" in the schools. The use of speeches, recitations, and songs was encouraged for the purpose of imparting to the children a knowledge of the state's resources, showing the material advance of the state, and sharing the patriotism, hardships, defeats, and victories of the people. Special attention was given to the motivation behind the heroism and sacrifices of the preceding generation.[75]

Some of the suggestions for inclusion on the "Mississippi Day" programs were: prayer; singing of "Bonnie Blue Flag;" an essay on Mississippi's resources; questions and answers from Mississippi history; a selection from "Christmas Night in the Quarters;" singing of the "Mississippi Ode;" Jefferson Davis's last speech in Mississippi; reminiscences of the war by a veteran; and singing of "America." It was also suggested that patrons and friends of the school be invited to visit on this day.[76]

Patriotism and citizenship were held before the student be-

---

[73] Jackson *Daily Clarion-Ledger*, 19 January 1903; Whitfield, "The Field of Activity," p. 6; Whitfield, "A Greater Mississippi," pp. 32–33.
[74] Jackson *Daily Clarion-Ledger*, 19 January 1903.
[75] Henry Whitfield, "Program for 'Mississippi Day,'" *The Mississippi School Journal* 6(1902):629.
[76] Ibid., p. 630.

cause the school had the responsibility of making good citizens. Whitfield wanted the children taught to vote from the right motive, respond eagerly to the call for jury duty, and to perform well all the ordinary duties and privileges of citizenship. The State Superintendent was critical of past civic instruction that was limited to cultivating political ambition toward the offices of senator, judge, and president. The new day in the South called for a wider vision of citizenship, and the teachers were challenged to make this one of the prominent goals of their work. Failure to educate students to perform all political obligations and position themselves with the highest civic ideals would be tragic indeed.[77]

Whitfield cited the exigent need for leadership in Mississippi to approach its responsibilities with clean hands, pure heart, and patriotic purposes. He preached that the motivation of patriotism should overshadow one's lust for position and power, and unselfish service to the state should be placed ahead of personal recognition. The Superintendent said, "I would have the school conducted as an organized society where rights and duties and reverence for authority will be taught by conduct." He appreciated the importance of knowing all about local, state, and national government, but at the same time he called for greater emphasis to be placed upon bringing the young people into the right attitude toward the government. One suggestion for accomplishing his goal was to tell the stories from history where individuals had sacrificed for their country.[78]

The educational program propounded by Whitfield encompassed the home, which was viewed as the foundation institution in society and the principal buttress of an organized social order. It was incumbent upon the school to emphasize such matters as the physical house, including its decorations and furnishings, teaching home industries to the children, and revealing the relationship between the home and other organized components of society. The Superintendent believed that the right kind of

---

[77] Whitfield, "The Field of Activity," p. 6.
[78] Whitfield, "A Greater Mississippi," p. 26; H. L. Whitfield, "Standards In Education," *The Mississippi School Journal* 14(1909): 26; Ibid.

homes could result only from the right kind of schools. He said that it was not desirable "to raise children without their getting a philosophy of home ethics." When speaking of an ideal home, he was speaking of a Christian home, where the Bible was read and every member of the family believed in God. A home of this type would naturally be characterized by patience, forbearance, and honesty. He reiterated his stance by saying, "It is one of the chief functions of the common schools to consciously give the students the right home ideals, and to see as far as possible that they develop towards these ideals."[79]

Wherever Whitfield traveled in the state, he sought to communicate to the parents the awesome responsibility of rearing their children. The parent was challenged to see the high purposes for which the child had been created. He had not been given to become a slave or animal of burden; neither was he in the world just to eat, sleep, reproduce, and die. The parents were asked to take a child in their midst just as Christ did during His earthly ministry, and inquire as to his purpose in the world. If left without guiding influence, the child would come in contact with things contaminating, and, if given no systematic training, he would become lazy and demoralized.[80]

In speeches for better schools in Mississippi, Whitfield would often refer to his childhood, and to his own educational background and the small schools he attended. He would refer to the boys who had sat beside him on a split log bench, and rhetorically ask, "Where are they today?" He would indicate they were in places of importance and then tell about each. With appropriate motions of the hands and movement of his bald head, he exclaimed, "They would not be there if it were not for education."

Even though Whitfield talked about such things as school buildings, curriculum, procedures, attitude, and community support, he concluded that only the teacher could make the desired school. In fact, he said the teacher was the school. Therefore, the

---

[79] Whitfield, "The Field of Activity," p. 6; Whitfield, "Standards in Education," p. 25; Whitfield, "A Greater Mississippi," p. 28; Whitfield, "Standards in Education," p. 25.
[80] Whitfield, "A Greater Mississippi," pp. 34–35.

teacher needed a vision before he could impart a vision; he needed training in order to communicate knowledge; and he needed a spirit of self-sacrifice since the material rewards were not sizable.[81] He, himself, was such an inspiration. Miss Winifred Welborn, well-known Mississippi educator, considered Whitfield "the greatest impetus Mississippi had for preparing teachers." Whitfield commended the Lowreys at Blue Mountain College for the splendid work they were doing in the field of teacher training.

The schools of Mississippi were an expression of the incentive, vitality, training, and industry of the teachers, according to Whitfield. There were those who believed the school made the teacher, but the progressive young leader believed the school could rise to the level of the teacher and no higher. Whitfield said that the teachers must accept the responsibility for the public feeling for the schools of Mississippi. When the citizens do not provide money, equipment, and personal time for the school, the teacher alone is guilty. He chided teachers who lamented when their patrons were not informed about school responsibilities and added that it was foolish to think these patrons were born with this knowledge or that the knowledge had been imparted to them in a supernatural dream. There was only one way a favorable question toward public education could be imparted, and that was through the teacher. People who have been set apart for the great and noble work of education must make themselves conveyors of this information to the patrons.[82]

Superintendent Whitfield concluded that the reason Mississippi lagged behind the more progressive states in education was that the people did not possess a workable knowledge of the purpose of the school. He was persuaded that there would be an urgent appeal for trained teachers, comfortable school buildings, and improved equipment, if the citizens could relate the school to the future of their children. Furthermore, the patrons would respond by having their children in school on a regular basis.

---

[81] Whitfield, "The Field of Activity," p. 8.
[82] Whitfield, "An Address by State Superintendent," pp: 135–136.

Therefore, the teachers were called upon to lead the people to believe in schools and recognize education of children as one of their most important responsibilities. In order to accomplish this goal, the teachers had to carry the message, since they were the only persons in the state whose work and interest afforded the opportunity of studying the philosophy of education.[83]

The teacher was given a two-fold responsibility: first, school work, and second, direct influence upon the patrons. The teacher could accomplish these goals by textbook scholarship, training, and character, but only if he had the spirit of a true teacher. Whitfield preached and practiced one of his favorite concepts—"No person can successfully teach unless his pupils are kept constantly in his heart." He told the teachers, "Your work will be judged more by the spirit that actuates you in doing it than the preparation you carry into it." [84]

The Whitfield paragon was held up before Mississippi teachers in the person of a little woman, weak in body, but strong in mind and soul. She accepted a school in one of the rural communities of the state only to find the building unusually depressing and equipped with antiquated furnishings. The only source of water supply was from the homes of the patrons several hundred yards away, and neither trustee nor patron had ever furnished a load of wood. The little woman accepted the challenge of the situation. She enlisted the children to help her enhance the appearance of the barren walls by using such items as pictures and flowers. She directed the cleaning of the grounds and enlisted a gardener to begin a definite program for beautifying the grounds. All of this resulted in a new interest and enthusiasm on the part of students and patrons.[85]

Unanimously elected for a second year, the little woman extended her vision beyond the school and grounds. Calling the mothers of the children together, she diplomatically explained the importance of the home in the education of a child. The mothers received a new concept of motherhood and proper con-

[83] Ibid., p. 136.
[84] Ibid., pp. 136–37.
[85] Ibid., p. 137.

32   CATCH THE VISION

ditions for correct child development. At the same meeting the teacher discussed school affairs and conditions and how these could be improved. Because of this woman's vision and enterprise the schoolhouse was enlarged and made more comfortable; good water was made available on the school grounds; and a second teacher was employed. Using this woman as an example of what a teacher should be and do, Whitfield claimed that any teacher with the same motive and spirit could accomplish the same.[86]

The State Superintendent was a strong advocate of the normal schools as a means of training teachers. In his first report to the state legislature he spoke of the normal schools which were conducted within the state during the preceding year. In addition to the regular week-long institute in each county, normals were conducted for white teachers in Batesville, Lexington, Columbus, Iuka, Bellefontaine, Winona, Crystal Springs, Fayette, Hebron, Biloxi, and Lauderdale Springs. Normals were conducted for Negro teachers in Greenville, Vicksburg, New Albany, Okolona, Macon, and Newton. These normals were financed by $2,500 appropriated from the state, plus $2,800 from the Peabody fund.[87] The normals afforded a great source of information and inspiration for the teachers.

An objective in the mind of Henry Whitfield was the establishment of a state training school for teachers. He revealed his thoughts by saying, "In my opinion the great need of our educational system today is a firstclass training school." [88] Mississippi had established and supported such a school for Negroes at Holly Springs, but there was no training school for white teachers.

By 1900 all states had some kind of public normal school. After 1900 a new phase of the normal appeared on the scene— the development of the teachers' college. A number of factors prompted this movement: a new respectability for education; a significant increase in high school graduates after 1890; a new interest in the quality of education; the demand for teachers with

---

[86] Ibid., p. 138.
[87] *Biennial Report of Superintendent* (1889), p. 2.
[88] *Biennial Report of Superintendent* (1903), p. 9.

the bachelor's degree; the growth of the normal school curriculum; and the rise of accrediting associations.[89]

Whitfield set forth four reasons Mississippi should establish a training school: to serve as a source of teacher supply; to supply teachers trained for their work just as other professionals were trained for theirs; to establish a higher standard of professional work; and to meet the unique educational needs of Mississippi. The vision of Henry Whitfield for a state training school did not become a reality until 1912, when the doors opened at Mississippi Normal College in Hattiesburg. "Among the leaders in this fine cause there was none who exceeded in earnestness, and persistency, Henry L. Whitfield," stated Dunbar Rowland, eminent Mississippi historian.[90]

Because some counties had conducted teacher examinations in such a manner as to permit unworthy teachers to enter the school system, Whitfield called for new regulations regarding teacher examination and certification. He wanted teachers examined on the elements of pedagogy, stating that "no one should be permitted to teach in our schools who has not to some extent familiarized himself with the great principles that have been worked out by the great teachers of all ages." The state legislature responded to this appeal by passing a law to strengthen the effectiveness of teacher examination and certification. Mississippi was falling in line with other sections of the country by giving emphasis to teacher examination. In 1903 90 percent of the teachers in Mississippi were not professionally trained, and 75 percent had attended only a rural school.[91]

The concern for trained personnel reached out to include the County Superintendent of Education. Whitfield wanted the legislature to do something that would make this office more effective. The salary was small and qualified men could not be found

---

[89] Butts and Cremin, *A History of Education*, pp. 449–51.
[90] *Biennial Report of Superintendent* (1905), pp. 8–11; Rowland, *History of Mississippi* 2:334–35.
[91] *Biennial Report of Superintendent* (1899), p. 6; idem. (1903), p. 14; Mississippi *Laws* (1902), chap. 110; Butts and Cremin, *A History of Education*, p. 453; Stuart Grayson Noble, *Forty Years of the Public Schools in Mississippi* (New York, 1918), p. 86.

34 CATCH THE VISION

who would devote themselves full time to the position. "The County Superintendent," according to Whitfield, "should be the most skilled and best technically trained teacher in the county." The legislature responded by passing a law to adjust the salary of this office. Whitfield also influenced the legislature to pass a law to adjust the salaries of teachers.[92]

The program of the State Superintendent called for the correction of weaknesses in the rural school. He wanted the children of the rural areas to enjoy the same opportunities as the children living in the towns. This seemed reasonable since the towns were able to offer certain advantages because of the support given to the taxable lists by the farmer. For example, every bale of cotton brought profit to the town where it was marketed; consequently, the towns were able to maintain better schools because of the contribution from the rural areas. Whitfield argued that the rural areas were the objects of discrimination and the future of the state depended upon the contentment of the rural people. Desirous of making available all the wealth of the state for educating all the children, he summarized his position by saying, "If the greatest good is to be secured to the greatest number, the greatest number must contribute through the agency of the State to the greatest good." [93]

In connection with the needs of the rural areas, Whitfield turned his attention to physical facilities and schoolhouses in particular. He informed the legislature that the schoolhouses were a disgrace to Mississippi, and the discomfort of the buildings resulted in lowered attendance. From 1900 to 1905 Whitfield gave special emphasis to improving the material equipment of the schools. He prepared instructions for the location of schools, construction of buildings, and healthy lighting, heating, and ventilation.[94]

In addition to the development of mind and muscle, the State Superintendent desired the development of aesthetic apprecia-

---

[92] *Biennial Report of Superintendent* (1903), p. 12; Mississippi *Laws* (1904), chaps. 165, 166.
[93] *Biennial Report of Superintendent* (1889), pp. 6–7.
[94] Ibid. (1903), p. 12; Noble, *Forty Years*, p. 67.

tion. Seeing the beautiful and making the beautiful would result in making a person more gentle and humane. Consequently, Whitfield believed that education was incomplete until a student's capacity to appreciate the beautiful had been cultivated. In order to enhance the aesthetic appreciation of the students, he wanted the schoolhouses to be exemplary in architecture, the walls decorated with beautifully expressive pictures, and all furnishings designed to produce a refining influence on the child. He concluded that once a person's life has been ensconced in the beautiful and the virtuous, he can never become completely corrupt. The legislature responded to Whitfield's vision by passing a law respecting the improvement of schoolhouses. The law did not fulfill all his dreams but it was a step in the desired direction.[95]

The State Superintendent of Education heartily endorsed and supported the new library movement in Mississippi. Superintendent G. G. Boyd of the Kosciusko school had inspired the formation of a school library association for the purpose of promoting established and circulating libraries. Whitfield also recommended that freehand drawing and vocal music be added to the curriculum. He believed in the refining influence of music and art, saying that "nothing contributes to the happiness of the people or brings out the better elements of their character than the love for singing, and the ability to sing intelligently." [96]

When Whitfield became State Superintendent of Education, the fall schools could not be opened before the first Monday in November. He challenged the legislature to change this, which it accordingly did. Whitfield anticipated permanent school districts and schoolhouse locations. Poor conditions had resulted from the authority of the county school boards to change the school districts and locate new sites for schoolhouses each year. Whitfield said, "A law for the permanent location of the schoolhouses would also have the effect of removing one of the most fruitful sources of neighborhood feuds, which so impaired the efficiency of the country schools." The legislature passed a law

[95] Jackson *Daily Clarion-Ledger,* 19 January 1903; Mississippi *Laws* (1904), chap. 121.
[96] *Biennial Report of Superintendent* (1901), p. 10; idem. (1903), p. 14.

related to school districts, but not in complete parallel to the Whitfield vision.[97]

Obviously the educational program envisioned by Whitfield would cost money. He said, "The policy of the State should be to require each county or school district to levy a certain tax for common schools and then supplement it from the State treasury to the amount necessary to maintain its schools for a given time." In other words, state aid should begin where local funds end. The State Superintendent was disturbed with those in the state who exerted more energy complaining about the conduct of the schools than in doing something about the situation. The people were reprimanded because they placed the needs of the schools so far down on their lists. In many instances all other needs were provided and then the schools were given the leftovers, if there were any. "Unquestionably," Whitfield said, "education is the best and most far-reaching return for . . . payment." Regarding the cost of education, he said that "education is the one subject for which no people ever yet paid too much. Indeed the more they pay the richer they become. Nothing is so costly as ignorance; and nothing so cheap as knowledge." The legislature increased appropriations for the schools from $1,000,000 to $1,250,000 during his administration.[98]

There were other features of Henry Whitfield's vision for Mississippi. He wanted the different institutions in the state to perform a distinctive work, thus providing a scheme of education with no competition among the institutions. He wanted Mississippi to have a complete telephone system and free rural delivery where each family could get a daily paper on the day of publication. All of this could result from proper education. A firm believer in the study of excellent literature, he did not want the children fed on the husks of common writings. He wanted to expose the young people to the choice writings by people of all nations and all periods of history. A first-class journal, devoted

---

[97] Ibid. (1901), p. 7; Mississippi *Laws* (1902), chap. 111; *Biennial Report of Superintendent* (1899), p. 4; Mississippi *Laws* (1900), chap. 116.
[98] *Biennial Report of Superintendent* (1899), p. 5; Whitfield, "A Greater Mississippi," p. 33; Mississippi *Laws* (1902), chap. 4.

State Superintendent of Education 37

exclusively to the interest of teachers, was promised by the State Superintendent; the publication of *The Mississippi School Journal* was the fruition of this vision.[99]

Under Whitfield's leadership, Mississippi made progress in eradicating illiteracy between 1900 and 1910. The percentage of illiterates, ages 10–14, dropped from 7.9 percent in 1900, to 3.5 percent in 1910. This progress compared favorably with Alabama, Georgia, and Virginia. Mississippi made greater progress than Louisiana where the percentage of illiterates dropped from 17.4 percent in 1900, to 11.5 percent in 1910.[100]

In 1900 the percentage of Negro illiteracy, ages 10–14, was 32.0 percent in Mississippi, 44.6 percent in Alabama, 36.0 percent in Georgia, 26.1 percent in Virginia and 49.1 percent in Louisiana. By 1910 the percentage was 19.4 percent in Mississippi, 27.5 percent in Alabama, 22.1 percent in Georgia, 16.0 percent in Virginia, and 41.0 percent in Louisiana. Thus Mississippi made approximately the same progress as Alabama, Georgia and Virginia. Louisiana continued to lag behind Mississippi in this area.[101]

In the matter of school attendance Mississippi made a noticeable advance between 1900 and 1910: 83.8 percent of the white children, ages 10–14, attended school in 1900 in Mississippi; by 1910 the percentage was 89.2. The national average in 1910 was 91.1 percent which was slightly higher than in Mississippi. In 1910 the average school attendance for Mississippi white children, ages 10–14, was higher than in Alabama, Louisiana, Georgia, and Virginia. In 1910 the average national attendance for Negro children, ages 10–14, was 68.6 percent, whereas the average for Mississippi was 70.0 percent. Therefore Mississippi slightly surpassed the national average in school attendance for Negro children, ages 10–14.[102]

---

[99] *Biennial Report of Superintendent* (1903), p. 17; Jackson *Daily Clarion-Ledger*, 19 January 1903; Editorial, *The Mississippi School Journal* 6(1902): 642.
[100] *Thirteenth Census of the United States* (Washington, D.C., 1913) 1:1231.
[101] Ibid., pp. 1122–25.
[102] Ibid., p. 1103; *Twelfth Census of the United States* (Washington, D.C., 1902) 2:xcv.

38 CATCH THE VISION

By the end of Whitfield's tenure as State Superintendent of Education, the state was spending approximately $5.50 on education for each enrolled child; this compared to $3.63 in 1900. The $5.50 per child compared favorably with Tennessee, which was spending approximately the same, and surpassed Georgia, which was spending less than $4.00 per child. However the figure was considerably below Virginia where the expenditure was over $9.00 per enrolled child.[103]

Whitfield felt that every village school should be responsible for dispersing the finest mental and moral culture to its pupils and should also be the hub of enlightenment, disseminating the accruements of a preferred culture throughout the total community. He viewed the school as the principal avenue of implanting in the minds of Mississippi youth a desire for the better things of life. He was convinced that intelligent citizenship results in a better spiritual man and a better spiritual man results in a better society.[104]

On 16 September 1923 the editor of the Jackson *Daily News* paid tribute to Whitfield in these words:

> With his broad vision as to the needs of the children of the state for better schools and more teachers, the new state superintendent traveled from county to county and preached his doctrine of education to the masses. It was his missionary work for schools which began a movement that afterwards developed an excellent system which in recent days has provided modern buildings with high-class teachers in the consolidated schools of the rural districts. Thousands and thousands of the rural pupils now have advantages which were barred in the day of Professor Whitfield to the city children. But both city and rural schools have shown wonderful progress. Whitfield today is seeing his dream in realization. . . .

Several months after Governor A. J. McLaurin had appointed Whitfield State Superintendent of Education, he was met by Robert Allen Whitfield on the streets of Westville. The elder

---

[103] *Statistical Abstract of the United States, 1901* (Washington, D.C., 1902), p. 426; idem., *1909* (1910), pp. 102–3.
[104] Editorial, *The Mississippi School Journal* 6(1902):642; Whitfield, "A Greater Mississippi," p. 29.

Mr. Whitfield very modestly and almost timidly approached the Governor to thank him for appointing his son to an important office. The Governor appreciated the expressed gratitude and replied by saying, "And he makes a good one." [105] Henry Whitfield did make a good State Superintendent of Education and was preparing to seek a third term in this office when he was invited to become President of the Industrial Institute and College in Columbus, Mississippi.

During the days at Steen's Creek Whitfield proved himself a worthy educator and school administrator as the school grew from sixty students to over one hundred. After his appointment as State Superintendent of Education, he visited every section of the state calling for school improvement. He was responsible for causing the people of Mississippi to place greater emphasis on the importance of public education.

Whitfield's mark on the educational life of Mississippi was left by his many accomplishments. He brought a new emphasis to vocational training, spurred the establishment of agricultural high schools in the state, and influenced the establishment of the textile school at Mississippi Agricultural and Mechanical College. Among other accomplishments, Whitfield opened the door for the acceptance of physical education into the school system of Mississippi, brought a new impetus to teacher training which resulted in the establishment of Mississippi Normal College in Hattiesburg, led in improvement of schoolhouses, set the stage for the creation of permanent school districts, and assisted the library movement.

[105] Robert Allen Whitfield, "Sketch of Henry Whitfield's Life," Robert Allen Whitfield papers, p. 2.

2 · President, Mississippi Industrial Institute and College

In the spring of 1907 Professor A. A. Kincannon, President of the Mississippi Industrial Institute and College, was elected Chancellor of the University of Mississippi. On 13 June 1907, Henry Whitfield was elected to succeed him as President of the first separate state-supported college for women in America.[1] Since it was then the vogue for the State Superintendent of Education to move to one of the colleges as President, there was nothing unusual about the procedure or precedent in Whitfield's going to the II&C. There was not a single dissenting vote among the board of trustees. Governor James K. Vardaman presided over the meeting and staunchly supported Whitfield for the position. The salary was $4,500 per year plus a residence on the campus.[2]

Henry Whitfield came to the Industrial Institute and College with definite convictions regarding an educational philosophy for the institution. Near the beginning of his tenure as college President, he gave a glimpse of his philosophy by saying,

> Education is now regarded by all authorities as being a preparation for life, and any subject which does not help to give the student a broader contact with life and a better mastery over the real problems of life, is lacking in educational value; in other words, education is now regarded as a scientific process with certain direct ends which should be consciously pursued. There are certain great fundamental ends which must be regarded in

---

[1] Jackson *Evening News*, 13 June 1907; Charles William Dabney, *Universal Education in the South*, 2 vols. (Chapel Hill, 1936) 1:356.
[2] Columbus *Commercial*, 18 June 1907; Jackson *Evening News*, 13 June 1907.

the education of every person who is to live in harmony with the institutions of the civilization in which he is to move. Among these are health, both individual and public; home; citizenship; industry; religion. These constitute the great institutions of a Christian civilization, and it is the great function of education to prepare the individual for the largest possible service in these spheres.[3]

A key word in the educational philosophy of President Whitfield was "practical." Convinced that too much emphasis had been given to subjects separated and removed from the lives of the people, he wanted education to begin where the college student touched life and to extend from there to more remote areas. "In other words," Whitfield stated, "the chief and first end of education is to adjust a person to the life that that person must live." [4]

Health was the first component in the educational philosophy of the new President. Whitfield always contended that the bodies of the students should be developed along with the minds, and he saw to it that the school gave equal attention to both physical and mental training. One of the popular notions of the President was, "A sound body for a sound mind." This philosophy of the importance of good health was also communicated to the students by means of certain pungent sayings, such as, "Keep your feet warm and your head cool." "The first end of education," according to President Whitfield, "should be the realization of a strong body. Without health there can be no high intellectual life." [5]

In 1909 President Whitfield, along with the presidents of Harvard University, the University of Chicago, and Leland Stanford University, appeared on the program of the Southern Education Association, meeting in Charlotte, North Carolina. Here he shared his concern for a greater emphasis on health by saying, "Look around and see the number of people, each of whom is ever carrying with him the incubus of a defective body, which is

---

[3] *Financial Report of the Industrial Institute and College 1909–1911*, p. 91.
[4] Henry L. Whitfield, "The Teachers' Reading Course," *The Mississippi School Journal* 14(1909):5.
[5] Columbus *Commercial*, 22 September 1912; Winston, *A Sampler*, p. 103; Columbus *Commercial*, 1 October 1907.

the prison house of the soul rather than, as God intended it should be, a mansion for a free spirit." [6]

Emphasis upon the home was a second precept which Whitfield fostered at II&C. He not only wanted the girls prepared to make a living, he also wanted them prepared to make a home. He spoke to the girls of homes that were "well located, properly planned, conveniently arranged, beautifully decorated, and perfectly sanitary." Speaking of his vision for a great South, Whitfield said, "a comfortable, beautiful, spiritual home, joined to a well kept farm with a diversified and scientific agriculture, is what I see in my vision for a great South." [7]

"The home is the fundamental institution of society," said President Whitfield, "and when our homes become in every respect what they should be, we need not fear the decay of society, nor the deterioration of any of the other institutions of our civilization." For a woman to venture into the business world was an honorable thing to do if necessary, but the greatest opportunity of full service for the average woman was considered to be in the home. Whitfield said, "I do not believe, as do some, that to be a wife and a mother is a limitation on a woman's possibilities." [8]

Citizenship was the third element in the Whitfield philosophy of higher education. The students were "daily becoming something rather than learning about things; . . . a knowledge of citizenship is a splendid acquirement, but to be bred by the school a citizen is infinitely better." Consequently, the emphasis was placed upon the natural performance of citizenship responsibility rather than just learning things about citizenship.[9]

> All who are informed must admit that in the face of our forty years of public schools that our civic life does not nearly approximate what it should be. The courts mete out justice to less than two percent of the murderers of the South; laws are

---

[6] Columbus *Commercial*, 30 December 1909.
[7] Ibid., 30 December 1909; Henry L. Whitfield, "Industrial Education," *The Mississippi School Journal* 14(1910):9.
[8] *Financial Report of the Mississippi Industrial Institute and College 1909–1911*, p. 96.
[9] Henry L. Whitfield, "The Teachers' Reading Course," p. 9.

not enforced; malfeasance in office is too common; our electorate is not well educated as to the duties of voters, school directors, jurymen, officers. In all parts of the South under different names, at times, have appeared organized bands, bound by horrid oaths, who go out in the night, to attempt to redress their real or supposed grievances in a manner that is a reproach to our civilization, and a menace to social security. The lust for office has displaced an intelligent patriotism, and our people have not had the opportunity for political education such as we should have had from those, who by endowment, training, and patriotism under normal conditions would have been our leaders. Schools should have furnished the antidote for this education by the demagogues.

This statement, recorded in the Columbus *Commercial*, 30 December 1909, reveals Whitfield's concern for the need of good citizens.

In connection with citizenship Whitfield emphasized the importance of service. This concept can be observed in the following statement about him.

> He brought . . . to his work certain definite and decided convictions as to the function and purpose of a school supported by the taxes of the people. The fundamental one of which was, that the reason for the being of such a school was not that a favored few of the young women of the State might receive a training and culture above the less fortunate many, but that through these the blessings they had received might be carried to and shared with others—in short, that through its graduates the II&C might become a blessing to all the people, a mighty power, reaching into every nook and corner of the State, for better morals, better health, better homes and better social conditions.[11]

The need was for a greater school that would help build a greater Mississippi. "If this institution fails to function as it should," Whitfield would say, "it has no right to exist." This philosophy was pertinent because one of the strongest arguments against equality of higher educational opportunities for women was that higher education was a luxury and did not merit tax

[11] Editorial, *The Mississippi Educational Advance* 10(1919):10.

support. Those who embraced this idea believed that higher education at public expense would be taxing the many for the profit of the few. They could not justify taxing all the people in order to support a college that only a privileged few would attend. Whitfield sought to answer this criticism by making all Mississippians beneficiaries of the II&C through its graduates.[12]

The students were told that when they received something they had an obligation to use it for the benefit of others. Whitfield sought to impress upon the students that the hard-working people of Mississippi were paying taxes to provide their education; therefore, they were committed to those who were willing to be taxed for the support of the school. He did not believe in education just for the sake of education; it must have a purpose and that purpose was service to others—those who had made it all possible. The President often said, "The people of Mississippi are giving you this privilege and you owe them something." Every effort was made to inspire the students with a feeling of responsibility to the state for their education. This concept can be clearly seen in the following statement by Whitfield:

> Every young woman who . . . accepts the bounty of the State should be made to realize that she is a party to an implied contract; that in consideration of what the State does for her, she agrees to be diligent in the performance of her college duties and that she will return to some part of the State and, with the better training she has received and the inspiration she should have received, carry the message of better living to those who were not so fortunate as to get this at first hand.[13]

"If you are here to learn how to back in and out [of] a parlor, or to any purpose other than service to the people," the President said, "you are wasting your time and the people's money."

President Whitfield was deeply hurt when one of his girls did not remain in Mississippi long enough to repay her debt. On one occasion he met a former student who had left the state to teach

---

[12] Miss Emma Ody Pohl, "Henry Lewis Whitfield, A Man of Vision," an address delivered 25 May 1928 at the dedicatory exercises of Whitfield Auditorium, Mississippi State College for Women; Butts and Cremin, *A History of Education*, pp. 368–69.
[13] *Financial Report of the* II&C *1909–1911*, pp. 92–93.

following her graduation from the II&C. The student was hurt when he expressed disappointment in her leaving the state to teach; however, she was offered a larger salary than could have been received in her home state.

A fourth ingredient in Whitfield's philosophical recipe for education at the II&C was industry. He stated that "the actual teaching of industry is so important that the formal side of education, when necessary, should be subordinated to it." In his first address to the faculty and students upon becoming President, he said, "The opportunity should be afforded here for a young woman to take any industrial art that would prepare her to make her bread or to adorn a home." Since work and service were the two products that paved the road to the abundant life, he taught that all the girls should be able to do something with their hands.[14]

A fifth feature in the educational philosophy of President Whitfield was religion. He believed that "every government, everything in life, in fact, is an absolute failure unless it is based on the proper relation with God." The girls were challenged to discover and develop their talents, then dedicate them to God. No student of the II&C could claim ignorance of the Whitfield concept that "the chief end of life is to honor and glorify God." In addition to receiving a solid academic education, he wanted the students to become fine women with high moral and spiritual character. It was expected that all of the girls should be able to stand up and say something intelligently in prayer meeting, and the President was disturbed when some could not even read the Scriptures with meaning.[15]

The emphasis on religion was not unique with President Whitfield but was a common concept at the time of his tenure at the II&C. In 1910 it was generally conceded that the character of the student was of utmost importance in both intellectual and ethical training. Teachers who were known to be immoral would not be

[14] Whitfield, "Industrial Education," p. 8; Columbus *Commercial*, 1 October 1909; Winston, *A Sampler*, p. 104.
[15] Mississippi Industrial Institute and College *Spectator*, 2 February 1919; Columbus *Commercial*, 1 October 1907.

permitted to occupy a place in the classroom; consequently, the example of their lives was considered more important than the instruction from a text.[16]

There were other concepts in the Whitfield philosophy that should be briefly cited, including the belief in the basic goodness of people. Most people, he thought, wanted to do the right thing and he never gave up this idea. Miss Marcie Sanders, Alumnae Secretary of Mississippi State College for Women, said, "He believed in people and believed actions could be influenced."

The President expected the students to take life seriously. He asked them to "get away from today with its shallow pleasures—look into the future—rise above the common herd and catch the vision." Whitfield was not opposed to pleasure and fun, but he cautioned the girls that they should not be interested in having a good time all the time. "There must be times of work," he said, "when you sacrifice a little present pleasure for something that's coming later." [17]

Whitfield's philosophy was questioned by the girls regarding his stand on dancing. During the first ten years of his presidency no social dancing was permitted. The students brought such pressure upon him that he finally gave in and agreed for them to dance one night per month, but without the presence of men.[18]

President Whitfield wanted to be broadminded but there was a limit to his tolerance. The students were welcomed to come to him with any problem and would receive a sympathetic hearing; however, there were certain matters that were unchangeable and the girls were expected to adjust to the situation. The girls were told that if they did not like being at the II&C then they did not belong there; they were expected to adjust to the situation rather than change it.

Whitfield did not want the parents to dictate the major of their children since his philosophy called for allowing the girls to find

---

[16] Charles Franklin Thwing, *A History of Education in the United States Since the Civil War* (Boston, 1910), p. 169.
[17] *Spectator*, 30 September 1917; 11 November 1922.
[18] Ibid., 5 January 1919.

their own places. It was his opinion that too many young people had been made unhappy because they were trying to please their parents in their choice of studies.

The first seven years under Whitfield witnessed remarkable progress in the physical improvements of the college. Within this seven-year period all but approximately five acres of the thirty-acre campus was filled or graded. The garbage dump was relocated and the old dump transformed into a beautiful garden where small plants, flowers, and shrubs grew. A new gymnasium, named for the President, and a new athletic field, providing a well-constructed running track with three and one-half laps to the mile, were constructed. A new library was completed in March 1908.[19]

Perhaps the most auspicious improvement was the construction of a new dormitory with appropriations made by the state legislature in 1910. This new dormitory, named Shattuck Hall, was constructed with four stories and furnished with modern accommodations and equipment. Kanahoah, the practice house of the Home Science Department, was constructed for practical instruction in homemaking. The name of this building was changed to Mable Ward Practice House in 1915. Over forty new pianos were added to the equipment of the music department and a pipe organ was installed in the chapel. In every possible way President Whitfield tried to make the facilities more comfortable and enjoyable for the girls. At the end of his first seven years as President, he said, "There is not a building on the campus that has not been either erected, completed, or repaired within the last seven years." [20]

In his opening address President Whitfield stated there would be no lowering of the academic standard and promised to expand the offerings of the school when means were available. The first year saw the reorganization of the Normal Department. The course of study in this department was extended to four years with the fourth year being coordinate with the sophomore year

---

[19] *Bulletin of the Industrial Institute and College* (May 1914), p. 6; (1908–1909), p. 80; (June 1912), p. 116; (May 1914), p. 6 (hereafter cited as *Bulletin* II&C).

[20] *Bulletin* II&C (May 1914), pp. 6–7; (June 1914), pp. 112, 116.

48 CATCH THE VISION

COURTESY MISSISSIPPI DEPARTMENT OF ARCHIVES AND HISTORY

President Whitfield shown with one of his sons at left and on the II & C campus at right

of the college course. The purpose of the department was to offer instruction in all subjects that were taught in the public schools of the state and to provide professional training in the history, theory, and practice of teaching.[21]

With expansion of the high school curriculum in the state, the Normal Department was eventually changed to a two-year course corresponding to the freshman and sophomore years. At the end of this study a student would receive a normal diploma. The state law provided that a student receiving this diploma and pledging to teach three years in Mississippi, two

[21] Columbus *Commercial*, 1 October 1907; *Bulletin* II&C (March 1910), p. 39.

of which had to be in rural schools, would receive a professional license to teach.

When the Normal Department was reorganized, a "model school" was set up consisting of the first four grades. Approximately thirty pupils were admitted to this school and the normal students were required to assist with the program. The Normal Department was abolished in 1918.

Henry Whitfield believed strongly in the development and care of the body; therefore, it should have been expected that he would organize a department of physical education. In his opening address before the faculty and students, the new President affirmed that "the course in physical education should never be elective, but every girl that matriculates here should be required to take physical training each day during the entire time at the college." Even at this time he envisioned a full-time director and adequate equipment for this department. Prior to Whitfield's coming to the II&C, the physical fitness program consisted only of an occasional hike to the Tombigbee or Orr Hill.[22]

A physical examination was given each student at the beginning of the year. At this time the college physician made a record of the functional condition of each student and included the degree of exercise that should be assigned to her. The director of the Physical Education Department made a careful physical measurement of each girl and listed all bodily defects. At the close of the year measurements were taken again in order to determine the progress made by gymnastic training. The work of the department was divided into three areas: practical training, athletics, and orthopedic gymnastics. The department sought to correct any minor deformities or physical imperfections which the girls possessed.[23]

At this juncture in the Whitfield story Miss Emma Ody Pohl must be introduced. The President was searching for someone

---

[22] Columbus *Commercial*, 1 October 1907.
[23] *Bulletin* II&C (1909), p. 60; Columbus *Commercial*, 22 September 1912.

to become head of the new Physical Education Department, and Miss Pohl, a teacher in the Greenville public schools, was invited to take the job. In "A Man of Vision," Miss Pohl recalls her visit with President Whitfield:

> Seated on the porch of his home in his favorite attitude, far back in the roomy wicker chair, head thrown back, his grey eyes fixed before him, he dreamed into the future. I wish I might give you some sense of the spell of warmth that I felt from the prospect of helping to work out that dream. His was the classic conviction that a sound body must house a sound mind. Nor did he believe that sound bodies for a handful of students who happened to have an inclination for athletics was enough to strive for. The whole of his little republic must be made fit, strong pliant muscles, well poised bodies, sound organs, ability to play certain games, an active play spirit, a love of play and exercise, definite health habits, high ideals of living, high standards of conduct. And as a result of these, if the leadership had been of the right sort, there should come better health—courage and initiative. With this equipment, they should be the more able, using his own words, "to touch life at every point."

Miss Pohl began her work by introducing such events as May Day festivals, folk dancing, and competitive games of various descriptions, but none of these involved campus-wide participation. She needed something spectacular, and the answer was the Zouave Drill, which she had learned from Count de Beauviere, French military drill expert. The drill called for color, flags, gay music, rhythmic exercises, campus-wide participation—everything she wanted. The Zouave Drill, first presented in 1912, became a tradition at Mississippi State College for Women.[24]

Miss Sarah Neilson, secretary to President Whitfield, said, "Nothing that has ever been done at the college has been more far-reaching in its effects than the introduction of the physical education program." Through this department the students learned to play together and the effect upon the spirit of the school was tremendous.[25]

---

[24] Columbus *Commercial Dispatch*, 1 June 1952.
[25] [Sarah D. Neilson], "History of Mississippi State College for Women," (Manuscript, Mississippi State College for Women) pp. 72, 73.

President, Mississippi Industrial Institute and College 51

The Whitfield years at II&C could never be disassociated from Miss Pohl. In a personal letter to her, President Whitfield expressed his appreciation and revealed her importance to his administration.

> I wish to give to you the expression of my gratitude for the enthusiastic support which you have always accorded me. I want to say to you that I do not think it would have been possible for me to have given the soul to the institution, which I believe it has, had you not been behind me at every step. It was your enthusiasm, your leadership, and your unselfishness that made it possible for me to accomplish what has been accomplished in giving the distinctive college spirit, which I think it is generally agreed that we have.[26]

The *Bulletin* of 1908–9 recorded the offering of a new course called Scientific Industrial. This was the beginning of what later culminated in the Home Economics Department of the college, which was established in 1915. At this time the home economics movement was gaining in momentum all over the United States. In the opening years of the twentieth century, courses in household economy were organized in the colleges of agriculture and mechanical arts throughout the country. By 1910 classes in cooking and sewing were taught in 142 institutions of higher learning, including state universities.[27]

One of the outstanding features of the Home Economics Department was the demonstration home, built in 1913, which provided a practical laboratory for practicing the art of homemaking. Here the students lived in groups of ten for six weeks, during which time each girl was responsible for doing the necessary work of the home. When asked why he gave so much emphasis to every detail of home life and home furnishings, Whitfield replied, "because people are to live in it."[28]

A department of Agriculture and Floriculture was established

---

[26] Henry L. Whitfield to Miss Emma Ody Pohl, 19 August 1920, in Pohl Papers, located in the Alumnae Office of Mississippi State College for Women.
[27] *Bulletin* II&C (1908–1909), pp. 30–31; Neilson, "History," p. 77; Willystine Goodsell, "The Education of Women," *Twenty-Five Years of American Education*, ed. I. L. Kandel (New York, 1969), p. 352.
[28] *Bulletin* II&C (June 1914), p. 117; Whitfield, "Industrial Education," p. 9.

II & C students working on the minature model farm

under Whitfield. This department included the study of soils and the principles of growing flowers from cuttings, seeds, and bulbs. Since agriculture was a required subject in a number of Mississippi high schools, President Whitfield wanted the II&C graduates to know how to teach it. This department was equipped with a small greenhouse and a miniature model farm located on approximately one and one-half acres of the campus. By this time the concept of the demonstration farm had become very popular and had revolutionized agriculture instruction.[29]

Physiography was another study introduced by Whitfield. Born of his theory that all the girls should be educated in the practical aspects of living, this course required the students to visit, observe, and report on various industries, farms, and natural surroundings. This study enabled the girls to learn how the people worked and produced in various jobs. President Whitfield personally conducted the girls on tours of a cotton oil mill, a gin, a brick factory, and a marble cutting factory in the area near Columbus. Along the way he would discuss such things as

[29] *Bulletin* II&C (June 1913), pp. 62–63; Neilson, "History," p. 71; Butts and Cremin, *A History of Education*, p. 448.

woods, crops, roads, road construction, materials, and the weather.

Another new offering in the curriculum was a study in the Bible. This course dealt with the Hebrew Prophets, Wisdom literature, the life of Christ, and the life of Paul.[30]

Whitfield continued to emphasize the importance and place of industrial education, and the college offered a certificate in this field. Here the student who could not attend the four-year program was given the opportunity of preparing herself for some worthy work. The offerings in this area included bookkeeping, stenography, fine arts, decorative and applied design, home science, dressmaking, and millinery. The industrial offering was ultimately divided into two courses—industrial and commercial. A certificate could be earned in either one of the two.[31]

The extension work of the college was also promoted under the presidency of Henry Whitfield. Schools and clubs were notified that the faculty members would be willing to do extension work within their particular fields by means of informal talks and lectures.[32]

Entrance requirements for the II&C were raised significantly under Whitfield's leadership. In 1907 the entrance requirement was seven units. The 1910 *Bulletin* listed the admission requirement as fourteen units.[33] In announcing this progress Whitfield declared,

> It affords me pleasure to announce to the Board that the entrance requirements of the college have been raised to the standard maintained by such great institutions as the universities of Michigan, Illinois, Wisconsin and the other great universities of the Northern states. We have the same number of hours of college work required for graduation. The time is now here when we should erect a no less high standard of efficiency for our schools than the people of any part of the world have. . . . There is no reason why Southern education should be any "cheaper" than Northern education.[34]

[30] *Bulletin* II&C (June 1913), p. 56.
[31] Ibid. (June 1918), p. 88.
[32] Ibid. (June 1912), pp. 122–23.
[33] Ibid. (May 1914), p. 10; (March 1919), p. 18.
[34] *Financial Report* II&C *1909–1911*, p. 99.

54 CATCH THE VISION

The faculty was strengthened during the Whitfield administration. At the time he came to II&C in 1907 twenty-two members of the faculty held the bachelor's degree and two held the master's degree. Out of the twenty-two with bachelor's degrees, nineteen were graduates of the II&C, while ten had no degree. In addition to these there were twelve music teachers, two having graduated from reputable music conservatories and the remainder having no degree. By 1914 considerable progress had been made in upgrading the faculty—one member held the Ph.D. degree, fourteen held master's degrees, and twenty-six held bachelor's degrees. Only thirteen of the bachelor's degrees were from the II&C. Eleven had no degree, but most of these were in the Industrial Department. There were eleven music teachers with three having graduated from reputable music conservatories. One method used to upgrade the faculty was the leave of absence. From six to ten faculty members took advantage of study in other schools each year. Low salaries made progress very difficult. In 1919 the President reported to the trustees that one-third of the places in the college were vacant, and he pleaded with the board to provide additional funds for faculty salaries.[35]

In 1911 President Whitfield employed the school's first dean. Under her guidance the system of keeping records was revamped and a new method of administering entrance requirements was introduced. The new dean was a helpful assistant to the President in improving the curriculum.[36]

The first social advisor for the II&C was employed during the Whitfield administration. After Shattuck Hall was built the President became concerned because of the lack of social training for the girls. Money was not available for the employment of a full-time social advisor, so an English teacher was em-

---

[35] Neilson, "History," p. 76; *Financial Report* II&C *1909–1911*, p. 103; Report of President Whitfield to the Board of Trustees of the Higher Educational Institutions of Mississippi (August 1919), p. 1, located in the John Clayton Fant Memorial Library, Mississippi State College for Women, Columbus, Mississippi.
[36] Neilson, "History," p. 71.

President, Mississippi Industrial Institute and College 55

ployed to divide her time between teaching and social advising.[37]

Prior to the coming of Whitfield as President of II&C, the school had neither adequate library facilities nor a professionally trained librarian. The academic life of the school was greatly augmented by the addition of a new library facility and a professionally trained librarian. In 1907 the library was reported to contain 5,500 books. By 1914 there were 9,000 volumes, 1,000 pamphlets, all the leading current magazines, and several daily newspapers. At the conclusion of Whitfield's administration the library holdings had increased to 13,539 books and 5,000 pamphlets. Miss Beulah Culbertson, long-time librarian at Mississippi State College for Women, gives Whitfield credit for the beginning of what is today an excellent library.[38]

As a result of President Whitfield's suggestion, a Teacher's Club was organized at the II&C for the purpose of studying and discussing questions of vital interest to the schools and teachers of Mississippi. Approximately 125 faculty and students attended each meeting. The club gave those who expected to become teachers an opportunity to learn more of their future work and develop a greater love for school work.[39]

During the first year of President Whitfield's administration the enrollment was 805, with only 333 of this number of college level. In 1920, the last year of his presidency, all of the 977 students were of college level. The number of college graduates increased from 23 in 1908 to 129 in 1917. There was a slight decrease in graduates between 1917 and 1920 because of World War I. The preparatory department was abolished in 1915.[40]

Between 1911 and 1920 the female college enrollment in Mississippi increased by 343. Since 225 of the increase was at the II&C, this illustrates the tremendous importance of the school to Mississippi. Whitfield claimed that over one-half the girls who attended college in Mississippi went to the II&C. The President was jubilant in the fall of 1917 when the II&C constituted

---

[37] Ibid., p. 89.
[38] Ibid., p. 86; *Bulletin* II&C (June 1914), p. 115; Neilson, "History," p. 86.
[39] "Notes From the Colleges," *The Mississippi School Journal* 13(1909):21.
[40] Neilson, "History," pp. 85–86.

the largest body of young ladies ever to gather at a similar institution in the South for a four-year course.[41]

President Whitfield worked diligently to acquire a large appropriation for the college. In 1908, with an enrollment of 805 students, the appropriation was $69,350. This compared to $74,178 for 354 students at Converse College; $51,396 for 292 students at Elmira College; $235,613 for 760 students at Mount Holyoke College; $72,854 for 427 students at Radcliffe College; $597,082 for 1,011 students at Vassar College; and $80,709 for 419 students at Bryn Mawr College.[42]

A member of the Appropriations Committee recalled how Whitfield came to him with tears in his eyes, earnestly pleading for help from the committee on behalf of the II&C. The President was honest in the amount of money requested for the school. He presented only the exact needs of the institution when requests from other institutions were sometimes exaggerated. Whitfield's concern for appropriations can be seen in the following letter to Governor Theodore G. Bilbo.

> In transmitting this budget for your consideration, I desire to state that there is a general feeling on the part of the friends of the II&C, especially the ladies of the faculty, that this institution has not been accorded even-handed justice by the State, as will be seen by comparison of the salaries here with the salaries of the other State schools. This statement is not made to invite any invidious comparison; no one more than the undersigned realizes the small salaries paid to the splendid workers in the other institutions.
>
> We also feel that so far as equipment is concerned we have been neglected. The report I am submitting shows that we have had little done for us in recent years. Notwithstanding the fact that our appropriation has been cut; that every scintilla of the preparatory department has been abolished—and ten years ago

---

[41] Comparison of figures in the *Statistical Abstract of the United States*, 1911, p. 109, and 1920, p. 108 (Washington, D.C., 1912 and 1923); Report of President Whitfield to the Board of Trustees of the Higher Educational Institutions of Mississippi (July 1917), p. 1, located in John Clayton Fant Memorial Library, Mississippi State College for Women, Columbus, Mississippi; Columbus *Commercial*, 27 September 1917.

[42] Columbus *Commercial*, 23 January 1910; Mississippi *Laws* (1908), chap. 7.

the preparatory department was practically the entire school—we now have nearly a thousand young women of college grade, which is probably the largest number of college students ever assembled in the South, I mean students pursuing A.B. and B.S. Courses.

I am glad to report that the institution is in good shape; the spirit of the student body is splendid, and we are longing for an opportunity to render larger service to the state.

I assure you that not only I but everyone connected with the institution will appreciate anything you may do that will help us to enlarge our opportunities for training and service.[43]

For the last year of Whitfield's presidency the appropriation was $102,092.52.[44]

President Whitfield introduced student government at the II&C. When he became President there was a harsh system in operation under which the faculty controlled the students by using demerits as punishment. This system produced good behavior but was not educating the students in matters of self-control and self-government. In 1910 a constitution and by-laws, written by a committee of faculty members and seniors approved by the President, were adopted. "Certain privileges were delegated to Student Government, others were reserved for the faculty, and the right to review all findings and activities and to change any part of the plan not functioning was held by the President. Responsibility for orderly conduct was placed upon the student body."[45]

A lyceum course, offered to all the students, made it possible for them to be exposed to great talent from all areas. Some of the features were: Axel Skovgaard, a Danish violinist; the New York Symphony Orchestra; Sousa's Band; The Russian Symphony Orchestra; Vanderbilt Glee Club; Theodore Bohlmann, noted pianist of the Cincinnati Conservatory; Millsaps

---

[43] Henry L. Whitfield to Theodore G. Bilbo, 23 November 1917, Theodore G. Bilbo Correspondence, John Clayton Fant Memorial Library, Mississippi State College for Women.
[44] Mississippi *Laws* (1920), chap. 5.
[45] Columbus *Commercial Dispatch*, 22 May 1950.

58 CATCH THE VISION

President Taft visits Industrial Institute & College—Taft is in center of sidewalk with Whitfield to his immediate left

Glee Club; Madame Jomeli, a dramatic soprano formerly with the Metropolitan Opera Company; and Alice Nielsen, prima donna soprano of the Metropolitan Opera Company.[46]

President Whitfield was always eager for his girls to be exposed to any informative feature. In 1909 he arranged for President William Howard Taft to visit the campus and speak to the girls. The students appreciated the visit from the President of the United States and enjoyed hearing him speak, but they were probably more impressed with his size and appetite—he ate five bowls of brunswick stew.[47]

Any person who attended the Industrial Institute and College during the Whitfield administration could never forget the chapel exercises. Occasionally a surprise guest would speak in chapel such as C. P. J. Mooney, editor of the Memphis *Commercial Ap-*

[46] *Bulletin* II&C (June 1919), p. 121; Columbus *Commercial*, 6 December 1908; 14 February 1909; 2 May 1909; 19 April 1914; 14 March 1915; 22 April 1915; 6 October 1918; *Spectator*, 28 April 1918; 3 April 1920.
[47] Columbus *Commercial*, 7 November 1909.

President, Mississippi Industrial Institute and College 59

peal; one of the Wright brothers who invented the airplane; or a local minister. Most of the time the speaker was Henry Whitfield. It was here that he propounded so many of his personal concepts and gave overall direction to the spirit of the school.

The paramount theme of the President was, "Catch the Vision!" He often referred to the Biblical admonition, "Where there is no vision the people perish." The girls interpreted this vision as related to self-improvement and service which would result in a greater Mississippi for the future. He would say to the students, "Girls, you are here with a mission to perform; find that niche you are to fill."

President Whitfield often read from the Holy Scriptures and gave an interpretation of the reading. He spoke of the methods of Jesus as a teacher and referred to Him as the perfect example of all times. There were several verses in the Bible which he delighted in using. One of these was I Corinthians 13. This chapter afforded him the opportunity of talking about God's kind of love, and he wanted his girls to exemplify the same qualities—patience, kindness, courtesy, humility, faith, hope, and endurance.

A second frequently used verse was Romans 12:1. This verse, presenting the theme of "reasonable service," gave the President a springboard from which he could launch a message on his concept of service. A third verse imprinted indelibly on the hearts and minds of the girls was Luke 9:62—"No man, having put his hand to the plough, and looking back, is fit for the kingdom of God." From this verse the students received a challenge on the importance of determination and endurance.

"Finally, brethren, whatsoever things are true, whatsoever things are honest, whatsoever things are just, whatsoever things are lovely, whatsoever things are of good report . . . think on these things" (Philippians 4:8) was another favorite Bible passage often used by President Whitfield. He wanted the girls to understand the importance of their thoughts; consequently, the test for correct thinking was presented in the words true, honest, just, pure, lovely, and good report.

"The wicked shall be turned into hell, and all nations that forget God," was used to emphasize the necessity of America's dependence upon faith in God. The students were also challenged by the statement, "So teach us to number our days, that we may apply our hearts unto wisdom" (Psalm 90:12). Through this verse the girls were reminded of the daily responsibility for the wise investment of their time in purposeful preparation for future opportunities. At the conclusion of some spiritual exhortation President Whitfield would remove his glasses, stretch out his arms and say, "Don't you understand?" Miss Ruth Hester spoke the sentiment of many former students when she said, "His talks in chapel will always be remembered because they helped to mold my character." Through the chapel messages the President knew how to "inspire the noblest and best within the girls." [48]

In the chapel exercises the girls received lectures on the image of the college. They were told never to do or say anything that would bring disgrace to the school. The President would occasionally ask the girls to whistle, or request to hear his favorite secular song, "Annie Laurie." Consistently he hammered away on the themes of gratitude, charity, clean living, exercise, student body spirit, pride in the institution, and civic pride in the campus.

If the students were too noisy when the President entered the chapel, he would say, "It is the empty wagons that make the most noise," or, "Shallow water makes the loudest noise." He did not like to hear the girls complain; therefore, the complainers were told, "Some of you came here with cockle burrs in your hair and are complaining—stop that! Appreciate what the state is doing for you."

President Whitfield emphasized the importance of sticking to every task until it was finished. Usually some of the girls wanted to leave the campus early before holidays. Because of this he would devote a part of the chapel exercise to speaking on the importance of remaining on the campus until the beginning of holidays. A favorite saying which he often used on these occasions was, "March right up to Appomattox."

The President maintained an exceptional relationship with the

---

[48] Columbus *Commercial*, 23 May 1909.

students as attested by the large number of alumnae willing to speak or write about him at present. At the beginning of his presidency he called for a meeting with a group of senior girls and sought their cooperation in helping him build a workable relationship with the entire student body. He had a fatherly attitude toward the girls and made it a practice to call each student by name when meeting her on the campus, often to the surprise of the student. Mrs. T. Jeff Walters, a student under Whitfield, said, "It was almost uncanny how he could remember every student's name, and even her family connections. Years after graduation he would meet a student and call her name." Every student knew that she had the genuine interest of the President, and he was loyal to his girls. Mrs. M. E. Page expressed the feeling of many students when she said, "I remember him with love and gratitude because he took a personal interest in making my college years happy and fulfilling."

The welfare of the students was placed above all other considerations by the President. One former student remarked that she could never forget his devotion and dedication to his girls. Every girl was treated equally and the students could not accuse him of being partial to anyone. He recognized the students as individuals and made each feel that she had worth and value in the world. If he were guilty of covetousness it was because he coveted the very best for his girls.

Whitfield was always available to his students, and they were welcomed to his office or home any time he was needed. Even if the family were eating a meal, the girls were free to come into the home with their problems. A choice illustration of this relationship was given by Miss Lillian Heffner. Facing her junior year Miss Heffner did not have sufficient funds to attend school and borrowed enough money for the train fare to Columbus. Arriving in Columbus she went immediately to the Whitfield home and set her suitcase on the front doorstep. The President came to the door and heard her story with patience and kindness. The conversation resulted in a plan whereby she could complete the junior year.

In 1919 a committee from the sophomore class needed a driver to take them into the country to collect greens for making the traditional magnolia chain for the senior class. President Whitfield came to the rescue by volunteering to drive the campus pickup truck for the girls. Wearing his old clothes, he seemed greatly to enjoy the outing as he advised on the choice of material that should be selected and assisted in gathering it. The one-hundred-yard chain was finished on time and many of the students never knew that the President had personally cut the vines and boughs for their chain. Two days later he presided over the baccalaureate service, where his appearance was of a different figure from the woodsman whacking away at smilax.

Many of the students did not have the financial resources that were required for a college education, but Whitfield tried to assist the sincere student in every possible way when funds were needed. According to Mrs. O. Z. Smith, a student under Whitfield, "many students would not have been able to continue in college if he had not made special concessions or arrangements for financial aid. I was one of this number and have been so grateful for his interest and kindness to me." Another student said, "As a blind student, I was encouraged by him to attend the college, though I had no braille books nor money to pay a teacher, but we believed a way could be found."

Never wanting to be a discouraging influence on the life of anyone, President Whitfield sought opportunities to encourage people. Mrs. H. Sam Lee, Jr., praised him for his encouraging influence when she served as president of the student government. Another student was rather dubious about singing a solo in the Sunday morning worship service of the Columbus First Baptist Church until the President spoke a word of encouragement. Mrs. W. M. Ledwith stated, "I was president of student government during my senior year and found him most helpful and encouraging." Interclass basketball games were a big thing on campus and each class had a mascot. President Whitfield was mascot of one class and seemed very pleased to attend every game to cheer and encourage the team.

The happiness of the student was always uppermost in the heart of the President. On one occasion when a student asked permission to change instructors, permission was granted because

President, Mississippi Industrial Institute and College

Whitfield did not want the girl to be unhappy, and he knew that some students could do better work under certain teachers. One Christmas several students could not go home because of distance or lack of money, so he organized the group into teams for a tennis tournament. The fun helped displace some of the unhappiness resulting from a desire to be with family at Christmas. In 1918 Christmas holidays were cancelled because illness had forced the closing of the school for six weeks. On behalf of the students the President wrote the following letter to Santa Claus.

Mr. Santa Claus,
North Pole

Dear Old Scout:

In so much as I have taken unto myself nine hundred and ninety-nine girls for the X-mas holidays, I take this means of notifying you that your co-operation in showing them a bully time is greatly desired by myself.

H. L. Whitfield [49]

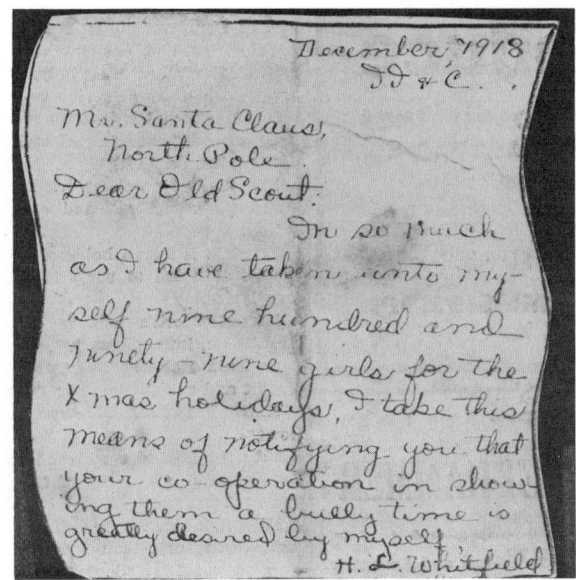

A letter to Santa from President Whitfield

---

[49] Mrs. Miles Hardy to writer, Tyler, Ala., 8 February 1971.

64 CATCH THE VISION

The 1908 *Meh Lady*, the school annual, was dedicated to Whitfield with the expression: "To our president Henry Lewis Whitfield for his broadmindedness and his big-heartedness, do we dedicate this, the seventh volume of Meh Lady." [50]

The students enjoyed singing the following song in the presence of their President.

II&C

Once there was a college in a Mississippi town.
It was the finest college that there was for miles around.
The girls that went to school there were the best that could be found.
It was the II&C.

We'll tell you 'bout our president, he's great in every way.
He makes you play at basketball and tennis every day.
He'll give you anything you want, if you will only say,
It's for the II&C.

Chorus:
II&C. double I and C.
A better school than ours
There simply could not be, rah! rah! [51]

There was a great loyalty among the students for him.

Henry Whitfield was a striking person in appearance and disposition. He was approximately 5'11" in height and weighed between 212 and 220 pounds; his head was bald and he wore a mustache much of the time. He was described as "a down-to-earth and folksy person, free from ostentation;" he was, "lovable, fatherly, yet firm." "He was optimistic, joyful and happy in his work." He always appeared to be in a good humor. Mr. Jim Eggers, prominent Columbus businessman, described him as "jovial . . . well-liked . . . one of the kindest men I have ever known." "You never saw him hurrying to or from any place, but he always managed to be where he was needed or expected."

Occasionally the President enjoyed smoking a cigar or chew-

---

[50] *Meh Lady* 7 (1908):5.
[51] Mrs. L. B. Llewellyn to writer, Baldwyn, Mississippi, 15 January 1971.

ing tobacco. He did not drink alcoholic beverages or practice the use of profanity. His taste in food was simple; he preferred vegetables, especially turnip greens, radishes, and corn bread. As he walked across the campus he would often pull pecans from his pocket and crack and eat them.

When President Whitfield traveled on the train, he often carried an algebra book, working algebra problems to pass the time. He had two favorite hobbies—tennis and golf. He could serve a swift ball and was considered to be a hard man to beat. Mr. T. E. Lott, Sr., one of the foursome in which he played golf, considered the President a pretty good golfer. Whitfield often carried a golf club with him as he walked across the campus and would hit at rocks and magnolia cones or pause for some putting practice. Any student who discovered him putting the ball was welcome to engage him in conversation.

Henry Whitfield loved his family and was very devoted to them. A student who was in his home many times recalled that he was a "thoughtful, loving and gracious husband and father." Meals were always preceded with a prayer of thanksgiving, and each morning found the Whitfield family engaging in a family worship time with Bible reading and prayers. At night the boys would listen as their father read to them, from either the Bible or other good literature. The father insisted that the entire family attend the worship services in the First Baptist Church of Columbus, where they sat in one pew together.

Mrs. Whitfield was a woman of small stature and delicate health. She was deeply devoted to her husband and the affairs of the home. "An absolutely devoted and unselfish wife made him free as few are free to devote himself to his life's purpose." Remaining quietly at home, she did not take an active part in community affairs and did not interfere with her husband's business as President of the college. The Whitfield home was characterized by gracious hospitality. Company was always welcomed; even students were allowed to enjoy the home by means of various social funtions.[52]

---

[52] Fant, "Henry Lewis Whitfield, Educator, Governor, Christian Gentleman," *The Mississippi Educational Advance*, 18(1927):313; Columbus *Commercial*, 24 May 1914.

President Whitfield could never get away from his love for the soil; therefore, he bought a small farm at Doolittle, near Newton, Mississippi. Here he spent a part of two summers with his family. The boys were not especially excited about the farm because they had to work hard, but the father thought the experience would be good for them.

The greatest personal tragedy that Henry Whitfield ever experienced came in 1916 when polio caused the death of his son, Henry Lewis, Jr. Robert Whitfield said this was the only time he ever saw his father cry. All of the sons were loved by their father, but possibly because Henry Lewis was named for him the relationship was somewhat different.

There are several delightful stories that illustrate President Whitfield's sense of humor. He always enjoyed participating in "Fun Night," an annual event when the faculty members entertained the student body. In one stunt he impersonated a phrenologist and undertook to examine the skulls of various faculty members. His original remarks were most entertaining to the students. When he came to a brilliant chemistry professor, who was suspected of wearing a wig, he shook her head, listened carefully, and announced that it seemed to be completely empty.

When the girls were leaving the campus for Christmas holidays the President told them to be careful and not to get bad colds. Then he added there were only two ways to get a bad cold; one was by eating too much and the other was kissing too much. Upon their return to the campus the girls discovered their President had an awful cold. Naturally they all wanted an explanation, to which he replied that he had not been eating too much.

Because of his sense of humor, the President was a good sport, which was appreciated by the girls. An annual event on the campus was the college circus in which students and faculty participated. One year he appeared on the scene as charioteer Ben Hur. His dress was a sheet draped over the shoulders; his chariot was the road drag which was pulled by the familiar and faithful old campus mule.

While Whitfield was attending a party sponsored by some of

the students, all were told to sit in a circle for the game of barnyard fowls. The President enthusiastically filled his place in the circle. One of the girls went around to each person supposedly whispering the name of some fowl. When the signal was given each person was to jump up and imitate the fowl which he had been given. Only the President was given the name of a fowl; the girls were told to remain quietly seated. When the signal was given, he jumped up alone and began to crow like a big rooster, much to the delight of all the girls.

Religion was always the indispensable feature of Henry Whitfield's life. His was a religion that found expression not only at 11:00 on Sunday morning, but every day and in every situation. He told the students, "We must take God in our plan, for if it is not worthy of God then it is not worth undertaking." "To know God and to do His will," he said, "is the one supreme end of human existence." An active member of the First Baptist Church in Columbus, President Whitfield served this church as deacon at the time a new sanctuary was constructed in 1908. For several years he taught a Sunday School class for the college girls, who considered him an excellent Bible teacher. He also taught the Baraca Class for men, who enjoyed his smooth flow of words and thorough Bible teaching.[53]

The President was often called upon to fill the pulpit in the Columbus First Baptist Church, and his sermons were considered to be among the best. He also preached in other communities and in churches other than Baptist. Vitally interested in the work of the Mississippi Baptist Convention, he enjoyed attending the annual sessions when possible. Evidence of his religious zeal is revealed by Mrs. T. E. Booker, who credits him with her conversion to Christianity during student days at the II&C.[54]

A person of civic vision, Whitfield took an active interest in

---

[53] *Spectator*, 2 February 1919; Mississippi Agricultural and Mechanical College *Reflector*, 23 January 1915; Henry L. Whitfield, "Standards in Education," *The Mississippi School Journal* 14(1909):29; idem., "The Teacher's Reading Course" 14(1909):9; *History of the First Baptist Church, Columbus, Mississippi, 1832-1964* (Columbus, 1964), p. 25.
[54] Columbus *Commercial Dispatch*, 7 February 1923; 14 November 1909; 23 November 1921.

the city of Columbus. He was a Mason, Shriner, and member of the Kiwanis Club. He was respected by the entire community, who called him Professor Whitfield. The community considered him an excellent administrator of the college and was proud he was there. He had a sincere desire to be a servant to the people of Columbus.[55]

A man of compassion, President Whitfield did many things for the underprivileged in the community of Columbus. A good illustration of this concern was the establishment of a free night school for those who had to work during the day. Designed for the less fortunate who did not have even a minimum education, the school was especially helpful to the mill village.[56]

Whitfield was instrumental in the organization of the Lowndes County Farm Bureau and served as its first President. He called upon the farmers to cooperate in order to make the Farm Bureau an influential and helpful factor in the county.[57]

The patriotic spirit of the President was especially evident during World War I. Several weeks of his time were contributed to delivering speeches in behalf of the war savings stamp campaign. He also offered to the senior class a special war course designed to assist them in meeting the conditions brought about by the war.[58]

There were dreams in President Whitfield's vision for the II&C that never came true; the most conspicuous of these was a farm for the college. For several years the trustees heard the appeal for a farm but continued to reject the project. Three reasons were given for the purchase of a farm. First, proper instruction could be given the young women of the college. Whitfield envisioned cottages on the farm with each having a garden, orchard, and poultry yard. Here the students could gain firsthand experience in the areas of dairying, horticulture, poultry, cooking, household management, and other farm-related work. The second reason given for acquiring the farm was to give

---

[55] Columbus *Commercial*, 19 March 1914.
[56] Ibid., 7 November 1909.
[57] Columbus *Commercial Dispatch*, 30 January 1921.
[58] Columbus *Commercial*, 30 June 1918; "II&C Notes," *The Mississippi Educational Advance* 7(1918):18.

worthy girls an opportunity of earning money for their education. Third, the farm would provide low-cost food for the college dining room.[59]

In 1918 Bernard B. Jones, a native Mississippian who had become wealthy, was visiting in Jackson, and heard the legislators in his hotel speak of President Whitfield as a man with a "foolish dream." Since Jones had also been called a dreamer of "foolish dreams," he desired an interview with Whitfield. "From this, and subsequent discussion, Mr. Jones caught a vision of service that might be rendered to the State. . . ." The possibilities of the Model Farm Homes, which the project would be called, excited B. B. Jones to the extent that he agreed to finance the entire project. He and Whitfield set out immediately to work for the realization of a "foolish dream." [60]

A 340-acre farm, located about two and one-half miles northeast of Columbus, was purchased, and Miss Frances Sale, a graduate of Columbia University, was employed to give direction to this new project. When the Model Farm was completed, the trustees refused to take possession. Records are rather hazy regarding this matter, but apparently the farm was refused because the trustees wanted to give a new direction to the school, and Whitfield was in trouble with the political powers of the state, though he was unaware of it at the time.[61]

Prior to the Jones farm incident, President Whitfield faced three crises during his thirteen years at the II&C. The first of these came in 1914 with the appearance of the S. T. Payer letter. S. T. stands for State Tax, thus State Tax Payer. Copies of the letter, containing a scandalous attack against Whitfield and his administration, were sent to members of the legislature, who were meeting in session at the time. Facts in the case are not clear, but there were those who believed Whitfield's emphasis on practical education rather than classical education brought him into

---

[59] Report of President Whitfield to the Board of Trustees of the Higher Educational Institutions of Mississippi (July 1917), pp. 2-3, located in John Clayton Fant Memorial Library, Mississippi State College for Women, Columbus, Mississippi.
[60] "Field Co-Operative Association, Inc., 1919-1946" (Manuscript in office of the Field Co-Operative Association in Jackson, Miss. pp. 53-54).
[61] Ibid., 55.

conflict with certain personalities who used the letter to vent their disagreement. "As a result of . . . its liberal attitude towards nonclassical curriculums, criticism was not infrequently directed at the college by educators of a more conservative type." The writer or writers of the letter were neither generally known nor publicly censured. Extensive investigation by the post office department did not connect any member of the faculty with the letter.[62]

When Whitfield returned to the campus from Jackson, he found hundreds of telegrams and letters of encouragement waiting for him, but far more important, the entire student body assembled in the chapel as a demonstration of their love and confidence in their President. It was a "tribute seldom paid to a man" and clearly indicated the student body's respect for the President.[63]

The *Mississippi Educational Advance* came to the defense of Whitfield by calling the statements false and the writer a fool. The First Baptist Church of Columbus adopted resolutions expressing the confidence of the congregation in President Whitfield. The President's gratitude for the widespread support which he received can be seen in the following letter:

My dear Mr. Street:

I wish to thank you from the bottom of my heart for your letter expressing your confidence in me and the dear girls under my care.

The splendid manner in which the students and the patrons of the institution have supported me is more than gratifying; not a student has withdrawn from school.

I am merely writing to express my deep appreciation; of course, the girls will give you the particulars.

Very sincerely yours,
H. L. Whitfield [64]

[62] George Duke Humphrey, "Public Education for Whites in Mississippi" (Ph.D. dissertation, Ohio State University, 1939), p. 278; Jackson *Daily News*, 31 October 1914.

[63] Mississippi Agricultural and Mechanical College *Reflector*, 17 January 1914.

[64] Editorial, *The Mississippi Educational Advance* 3(1914):2; *Reflector*, 17 January 1914; H. L. Whitfield to J. W. Street, 13 January 1914, filed in Whitfield Scholarship folder of the Mississippi State College for Women Alumnae Office.

The second crisis followed almost immediately upon the heels of the Payer letter. President Whitfield did not renew the contracts of four faculty members for the fall term of 1914. No explanation was given as to why these ladies should not be returned to the faculty, and there was vociferous disapproval of this action. One state legislator questioned the wisdom of such action, especially in light of occurrences resulting from the Payer letter.[65]

Governor Earl Brewer sensed a concerted movement to force the retention of these faculty members, but he refused to intervene and supported Whitfield's position. T. B. Franklin, member of the Board of Trustees of the II&C, supported the President by saying, "His action in this matter has my fullest approval." O. F. Lawrence, secretary of the trustees, also supported Whitfield, but held out hope for the four ladies by commenting, "If these persons can persuade Mr. Whitfield to recommend them . . . the Trustees will reelect them." Two of the teachers returned to the faculty in the fall of 1914 but the other two never returned.[66]

This crisis points up some evident conflict between Whitfield and certain members of the faculty, but in general the relationship between president and faculty was most cordial. Miss Etta Atwell enjoyed her relationship with him, while Miss Nellie Keirn, another faculty member, concluded that "in the main, faculty and students were loyal to him."

The third crisis of the Whitfield administration came in 1920, when the legislature gave serious consideration to the possibility of creating one state university that would absorb the other state-supported colleges. This move would have signaled the end of the II&C as a separate institution in Columbus. The President worked diligently to defeat this proposal. First, he invited sixty members of the House and Senate to visit the campus and learn

---

[65] Dr. James Ruffin to H. L. Whitfield, 26 June 1914, Rice Collection, Mitchell Memorial Library, Mississippi State University, Special Collections.
[66] Ibid., Earl Brewer to Nannie Herndon Rice, Sidney Gay, and Maude Carpenter, 27 June 1914; O. F. Lawrence to Nannie Herndon Rice, 6 June 1914; Neilson, "History," p. 77.

72 CATCH THE VISION

the significance of the II&C. The meeting was successful since many of them pledged their support to retain the college.[67]

The second phase of Whitfield's strategy was to enlist renowned educators in his support. Three of these will serve as illustrations. Dr. F. G. Bonser, Professor of Industrial Education, Teachers College, Columbia University, wrote:

> I am indeed sorry that your splendid institution is under the necessity of fighting for its life. In my visit of several days to your school, and in my acquaintance with graduates and the work they are doing, I have come to appreciate the great contribution your school has made and is making to the educational life, home life, and social life, of Mississippi. You have done a work such as no mere normal school could do and such as no state university has done. The peculiar genius of President Whitfield has shown itself in his sensing the most vital and fundamental needs of the women, homes, and schools of your state and adapting the work of the Institute and College to meeting these needs. I know of no other school, South or North, that has been more signally successful in realizing the genuine needs of the people who support it. It would be unfortunate, indeed, to curtail the possibilities of the school by reducing the scope of its work.[68]

Dr. M. V. O'Shea, Professor of Education, University of Wisconsin, came to the defense of the school by sharing his regard for the II&C. Speaking of Whitfield he said, "I have often marveled at his insight into educational conditions and ways and means of making educational subjects and educational methods of genuine practical value to those who are preparing to teach." Dr. O'Shea called Whitfield, "The Pestalozzi of Mississippi." [69]

F. M. Brawley, President of the College of Industrial Arts, Denton, Texas, spoke of the II&C as one of the great colleges of the South because of the fine training and unusual teaching ability of the graduates. The statements of these three educators

---

[67] Neilson, "History," p. 91; Columbus *Commercial Dispatch*, 22 February 1920.
[68] *Spectator*, 21 February 1920.
[69] Ibid.; M. V. O'Shea, "A Modern Pestalozzi," *The Wisconsin Journal of Education* 43 (1911):92.

not only enhanced the reputation of the college but also gave insight into the personal reputation of Henry Whitfield among the leaders in education.[70]

President Whitfield came through the crisis victoriously and the battle wounds were soothed when the legislature voted not only to defeat the proposal of one university but also to change the name of II&C to Mississippi State College for Women. This had been another dream of the President. The victory was short-lived because Whitfield received the following letter in July, 1920.[71]

> President H. L. Whitfield
> Mississippi State College for Women
> Columbus, Miss.
>
> Dear Sir:
>
> At a regular meeting of the Board of Trustees of Colleges and University Dr. J. C. Fant was elected President of the Mississippi State College for Women for the session 1920–1921.
>
> The Board understands that your time expires on October 1, 1920 and they have given you a leave of absence from and after August 1, 1920 to October 1, 1920, with full pay, provided you will leave someone to look after executive matters.
>
> Dr. Fant has been requested by the Board of Trustees to take charge on September 1, 1920, and he will be on hand at that time.
>
> Very truly yours,
> A. B. Schauber [72]

The students were shocked to learn their President had been dismissed. The dismissal, which was a surprise to Whitfield, was evidently related altogether to a matter of politics. When Lee Russell was seeking the office of Governor in 1919, the President received a letter from Theodore Bilbo stating that the college faculty would be expected to "get in line" with Russell and

---

[70] *Spectator*, 21 February 1920.
[71] Mississippi *Laws* (1920), chap. 256; Neilson, "History," p. 91; The name of the school was changed to Mississippi University for Women in 1974.
[72] A. B. Schauber to H. L. Whitfield, 24 July 1920, in the A. B. Schauber correspondence of the John Clayton Fant Memorial Library, Mississippi State College for Women.

support him. Whitfield refused to cooperate in this political intrigue; consequently, he was dismissed when Russell became Governor.[73]

Approximately four weeks following the dismissal, Whitfield spoke in the First Baptist Church of Columbus. After thanking the people for their encouragement and expressions of confidence, he gave no evidence of either discouragement or despondency as he spoke of greater and enlarged service for the Master.[74]

Whitfield's response to the dismissal can be seen in the following excerpt from a personal letter.

> I am sure that all friends of mine will take the same view of the situation that I do. It is not what is done from the outside that affects us, but it is our attitude towards what is done. I know you will all accord the new administration cordial and enthusiastic support and that you will do what you can to make the MSCW grow into a greater power and larger influence for everything affecting the welfare and honor of not only the women of the state but of every interest in the state.[75]

The accomplishments of the Whitfield administration have already been cited, but those who remember him best agree that the greatest contribution was his influence in the lives of the students. The following testimonies will serve to illustrate this.

> I am sure the molding of character with his inspiration and chapel talks left ambitions in the hearts of all girls who attended II&C. I know it did on mine.[76]

> My husband and I were both teachers in small towns and communities of Mississippi for a period of about fifty years. During this time I was often reminded of things that Mr. Whitfield said about problems that we met in several parts of Mississippi where we worked, and was enabled to be more patient and more able to help than I might have been without Mr. Whitfield's influence on my life.[77]

[73] Columbus *Commercial Dispatch*, 1 August 1920.
[74] Columbus *Commercial Dispatch*, 18 August 1920.
[75] H. L. Whitfield to Miss Emma Ody Pohl, 19 August 1920, Pohl Collection, Mississippi State College for Women Alumnae Office.
[76] Mrs. Connie McCain to writer, Houston, Mississippi, 11 January 1971.
[77] Mrs. C. R. Stephens to writer, Brooksville, Florida, 13 January 1971.

President, Mississippi Industrial Institute and College 75

Whatever I have been able to accomplish and complete, I owe to President Whitfield and to my Father.[78]

Through the teaching of President Whitfield I have been interested in my home town Monroe, Louisiana. I have been a member and served as President and officer of many organizations, some of which I was an organizing member.[79]
I have never forgotten his influence, and all my life I have been busy with good works and this started with the Whitfield influence.[80]

In 1933 I was chosen by Duval County and the U.S. Office of Education to begin a course of Cooperative Vocational Education for high school seniors and juniors. It was the first in the nation and proved most successful. For the next 30 years I worked as supervisor of the program here and trained coordinators as a member of the University of Florida in the summer. I felt that the philosophy and broad background of Mr. Whitfield was a contributing factor in my success.[81]

In August 1920 Whitfield was unanimously elected principal of the Bolivar County Agricultural High School, William Hull having resigned this position to become President of Mississippi Agricultural and Mechanical College. Whitfield declined the offer because he felt honor bound to care for the Jones farm; therefore, the Whitfield family moved to the farm.[82]

Whitfield first offered the farm to Lowndes County to be used as an agricultural high school, but the proposition was rejected. Because of the overcrowded conditions in the Masonic Orphanage in Meridian, the Jones farm was offered to the Masons to be used as a home for orphaned boys. The offer was accepted, Whitfield was appointed superintendent, and the first contingent of twenty-eight boys arrived on 5 June 1921. Eventually there were approximately sixty boys under his care. During his presidency at the II&C, he had spoken of his dreams and hopes for orphaned boys. "He wanted the best possible sur-

[78] Mrs. Clarence O. Pollard to writer, Hemet, California, 30 January 1971.
[79] Mrs. W. C. Oliver to writer, Monroe, Louisiana, 30 January 1971.
[80] Conversation with Mrs. Claudia Whitney, Jackson, Mississippi, 13 November 1970.
[81] Mrs. Anne H. Franz to writer, Jacksonville, Florida, 25 January 1971.
[82] Columbus *Commercial Dispatch*, 4 August 1920; 11 August 1920.

roundings for them, believing that environment affected very strongly their behavior and character." In all probability the interest in orphaned boys was heightened because of the bitter experiences of his father.[83]

Whitfield wanted the boys to learn a trade while receiving their education. The hours from eight to twelve each morning were devoted to the study of books with Whitfield as the teacher plus occasional help from the students at MSCW. The afternoons were given to various responsibilities about the farm. There were hogs, chickens, cows, and horses to attend, in addition to the garden and crops of corn and oats. Just enough cotton was grown to teach the boys how to do it. He did not send the boys out to work; he led them, and he did not expect them to do any more than he.

The Superintendent was concerned that the boys receive a balanced diet each day. Most of the food was grown in abundance on the farm. Whitfield took the surplus food to MSCW, where the girls were impressed and grateful as they saw him, dressed in overalls and straw hat, drive a truck to the kitchen door and unload fresh vegetables. On one occasion, when a large field of peas was ready to gather, he called upon the college girls to don their bloomer gym suits and come to his aid.

The religious training of the boys was always uppermost in the mind of Henry Whitfield. All of them went to the Columbus First Baptist Church each Sunday for worship. A Wednesday night service was conducted at the farm, with Whitfield as the speaker and teacher. The boys were encouraged to memorize one verse of Scripture each week.

Several statements from men who lived in the orphanage at the time will reveal their attitude toward Whitfield.

> I liked him . . . a fine man . . . all the boys liked him.
>
> In spite of the fact that he was daily confronted with a very mischievous and somewhat "hardened" group, he was always the recipient of our greatest respect.
>
> I think he was as good a man as ever lived.

[83] Ibid., 6 December 1920; 24 April 1921.

President, Mississippi Industrial Institute and College

The boys loved him.

All the boys liked Mr. Whitfield as he was trying to make a real home for us.

I look back now and recall any number of times he taught us self reliance by requiring us to do jobs that were not exactly familiar to us.

I am confident that I speak for all the boys when I say that Gov. Whitfield was understanding, kind and loving to all the boys under his care.

Not only the boys, but others recognized and appreciated Whitfield's accomplishments at the orphanage. The board of managers for the B. B. Jones Masonic Farm School came for their first inspection and "complimented Superintendent Whitfield very highly on his work." [84]

After he had performed great service at Mississippi State College for Women and the B.B. Jones Masonic Farm School, another door was about to open for Henry Whitfield. Much to the surprise of his family and many friends, he offered himself as candidate for Governor of Mississippi. This announcement for the office of Governor came as a surprise because he apparently had taken no serious part in politics since becoming President of the college. It appears that one can safely say that he offered himself as candidate for Governor simply because of his love for Mississippi and desire to serve the people.

[84] Columbus *Commercial Dispatch*, 24 August 1921.

3 · Governor of Mississippi

Henry L. Whitfield was first suggested as a prospective candidate for Governor in 1909, but he denied any desire to enter the campaign, much to the delight of Columbus citizens who wanted him to remain as President of the II&C.[1] Approximately one year later the rumor persisted as personal friends urged him to enter the race. The pressure was so great that he seriously considered the move. Having traveled over the entire state as State Superintendent of Education, he was probably known by more people than any other man in the state; this exposure would have been invaluable in a state campaign. After serious consideration he decided not to enter the race for Governor at that time.[2]

In 1921 the editor of the Columbus *Commercial Dispatch* presented Whitfield as a potential candidate for Governor without knowing if he would consent to make the race. "We believe he is the most logical man in the state for the Governorship," the editorial stated, "and we believe, further, that if the sentiment of the people is sufficiently focused on him he will make the race."[3]

On 17 June 1922, Whitfield formally announced his candidacy for Governor of Mississippi. The official statement opened with the following remarks.

> I am a candidate for the office of Governor, subject to the action of the Democratic primaries of nineteen twenty-three.

[1] Columbus *Commercial*, 21 November 1909.
[2] Jackson *Daily News*, 8 May 1910.
[3] Columbus *Commercial Dispatch*, 3 July 1921.

From every section of the state voluntary information has come to me which makes me believe that the people are now willing and anxious to unite without regard to past divisions, in one common effort to bring about better social and industrial conditions in the state. In this get-to-gether spirit for the welfare and honor of the state, I am making this announcement for the highest office in the gift of the people. If elected I want to here and now promise the people of Mississippi that so far as I know my duty, I shall be true to the state's best interest. I want to furthermore promise the people, that in the event of my election, I shall always endeavor to decide all questions for the best interest of the State of Mississippi without regard to personal relationship. It will be my great ambition, if elected, to be Governor of all the people without reference to the fact as to who supported me.[4]

The announcement touched a number of other matters such as taxation, industrial development, farming, timber, schools, health, and law and order.[5]

Though expected by some, others were surprised to learn of Whitfield's interest in seeking the Governor's office. Early in 1922 his father was convinced that he would not seek the office of Governor, as evidenced in the following letter.

Henry is not seeking the office of governor at the coming election, but quite a pressure is being brought to bear to get him to run for the office. Since the present administration of Mississippi state politics is a shameful affair, it appears that almost any good democrat—not of the Vardaman, Bilbo or Russell stripe, can easily be elected now, as we may suppose that the good men who voted for Russell are now too disgusted to vote again for any of his party stripe.[6]

R. A. Whitfield, a son, was very much surprised when his father announced for the office. Mrs. C. M. Kolb, a former student at II&C, stated that she was also surprised to hear that he was considering the campaign since he never gave the appearance of being interested in such an undertaking. Miss Etta At-

[4] Ibid., 18 June 1922.
[5] Ibid.
[6] R. A. Whitfield to Mary Massey Whitworth, 15 March 1922, Whitworth Scrapbook, Pickens, Miss.

well, a member of the II&C faculty, observed that he never did anything as President of the college to maneuver himself into a political advantage or to indicate an interest in the office of Governor.

In addition to Whitfield, there were four other personalities in the 1923 campaign—Theodore Bilbo, former Governor; Lester Franklin, a member of the State Senate; Sennett Conner, Speaker of the House of Representatives; and Judge Percy Bell. The campaign ultimately became a contest between Whitfield and Bilbo. Franklin was weakened by the personal endorsement of Governor Lee Russell, who had been discredited in the eyes of the state by the famous Birkhead trial. Franklin and Conner became embrawled in private debates which hurt each of them. Percy Bell was never a real threat in this campaign. With the elimination of Franklin, Conner, and Bell in the first primary, Whitfield and Bilbo were left to contend for the Governor's chair.[7]

There were eight obvious planks in the Whitfield platform.[8] First, he promised equal rights to all and special privileges to none, with a square deal for every citizen. This statement was apparently necessary because he had been accused of appealing to the upper-class element. Second, emphasis was given to economy in government. He promised to put the state on a "pay as you go" basis, without imposing additional tax burdens upon the people. This plank was evidently inserted because the expenditures of the previous eight years had been more than the income, thus leaving the state in an unenviable financial situation.[9]

Third, Whitfield called for profitable farming. Convinced that too many people were leaving the state because farming had become unprofitable, he promised help primarily through an intelligent system for marketing farm products. He often carried

---

[7] Memphis *News Scimitar*, 29 July 1923; Grenada *Sentinel*, 27 July 1923 (the Birkhead case is discussed below in this chapter); Jackson *Daily News*, 13 June 1923.

[8] Except where otherwise noted, the platform is taken from the Meridian *Star*, 22 August 1923.

[9] John K. Bettersworth, *Mississippi Yesterday and Today* (Austin, 1964), p. 289; Jackson *Daily News*, 21 March 1926.

different types of containers to illustrate the lack of uniformity in marketing farm products.

Fourth, new capital would be welcomed into the state, thus developing the state's resources and increasing the tax base. Whitfield opposed the exploitation of the state's resources and opportunities by special interest groups but wanted to be a friend to honest business. Capital and labor were promised opportunity without fear if the laws were obeyed.

The fifth plank called for removing the educational institutions from politics. Teachers were promised that they would be selected on the basis of qualifications and service rather than politics. This theme became a major issue since he had been removed from the presidency of II&C because of political chicanery.[10] In order to emphasize the importance of this particular plank, he often exclaimed,

> It will always be a source of pride to me and a heritage to my children, that when I was ordered to "line up" the influences of the Mississippi State College for Women, for a candidate for governor, then a trustee, and now the governor of the state, I had the moral courage to say that I would lose my position as president of that institution rather than to make it the servile instrument by which the institution, dedicated to the noble young womenhood of the state, should be forced into the filth and mire of the then Mississippi politics.[11]

Sixth, Whitfield promised to "accord the noble women of our state a most earnest support in their effort to banish social diseases from Mississippi and to safeguard our splendid boys and girls." [19] When he called on Joe Cook, President of Mississippi Normal College at Hattiesburg, to enlist his support in the campaign, they both agreed that the female vote could make the difference between defeat and victory. This plank was obviously designed to attract the support of the women voters.[12]

The seventh plank called for more effective law enforcement. Whitfield especially promised to suppress the whisky traffic in

---

[10] Brandon *News*, 31 May 1923.
[11] Meridian *Star*, 22 August 1923.
[12] Ibid.

the state and refuse parole to those convicted of violating the prohibition laws. In the eighth plank of his political platform he simply promised never to embarrass the people of Mississippi, an obvious reference to Bilbo, Russell, and the Birkhead affair.

There were ten planks in the political platform of Theodore Bilbo.[13]

> 1. Retention of the present law regarding the State Revenue Agent.
> 2. Reform of the affairs of some of the State institutions, thus placing them on an economical business basis.
> 3. Strict enforcement of all laws, especially the prohibition laws.
> 4. Establishment of a central purchasing agency for all state institutions, including the colleges and penitentiary.
> 5. Creation of a state marketing bureau.
> 6. Creation of a bureau of information designed to collect and dispense definite geological information regarding the resources of the state.
> 7. Continuation of road construction.
> 8. Enactment of a law whereby the family of penitentiary convicts and the families of victims of criminal acts could receive from ten to fifty percent of the pro rata earnings of the respective convicts.
> 9. Establishment of a printery by the state for printing school books and record books.
> 10. Establishment of a hospital for north Mississippi.

In connection with plank number seven, Bilbo proposed that convict labor be used to make the vitrified brick for road paving. The political platforms of Bilbo and Whitfield were closely paralleled except for two distinctions. Bilbo omitted any reference to opened doors for outside capital and made no mention of the women.[14]

Convinced that citizens of Mississippi had been "surfeited on vile political slush" in recent years, Whitfield promised a clean campaign:

> It is my purpose to make as clean a campaign as can be waged; if there is anything wrong in the lives of my opponents it will be for the voters of Mississippi to find out, as I do not intend to

---
[13] Pontotoc *Sentinel*, 10 May 1923.
[14] Raleigh *Smith County Reformer*, 28 June 1923.

bring forth their skeletons to rattle them before the people of the state. I propose to wash no soiled linen in this canvass.

I am appealing to the patriotic liberty loving men and women who love their state, who want to see better conditions obtain and who place the good of the state above selfish interests, and who stand for the interest and honor of the state rather than for their own greed and selfishness.[15]

Whitfield waged a vigorous campaign for the state's highest office. Within one week he appeared in the counties of Simpson, Jefferson Davis, Smith, Jasper, Jones, Lauderdale, Kemper, Winston, Noxubee, Oktibbeha, and Webster. Following is a typical schedule of engagements for four days.[16]

Wednesday, July 25
 Tupelo (Lee County)—11 am
 Guntown (Lee County)—2 pm
 Booneville (Prentiss County)—8 pm
Thursday, July 26
 Ripley (Tippah County)—11 am
 Ashland (Benton County)—2 pm
 Potts Camp (Marshall County)—8 pm
Friday, July 27
 Oxford (Lafayette County)—11 am
 A. M. Taylor (Lafayette County)—2 pm
 Grenada (Grenada County)—8 pm
Saturday, July 28
 Cascilla (Tallahatchie County)—10 am
 A. M. Teasdale (Tallahatchie County)—2 pm
 Oakland (Yalobusha County)—4 pm

Even in the face of a demanding schedule, poor roads, and hot weather, Whitfield never missed an appointment. While he was speaking in Jackson's Poindexter Park, a case of laryngitis made communication difficult, but he refused to stop for rest. An automobile accident on the Pocahontas road near Jackson resulted in severe bruises, but he continued the journey to the next speaking engagement.[17]

[15] Brandon *News*, 31 May 1923; Jackson *Daily News*, 25 April 1923.
[16] Columbus *Commercial Dispatch*, 25 July 1923.
[17] Harry Bryan Scrapbook 1:8. Prepared by Harry Bryan, Whitfield's campaign manager, this scrapbook contains a wealth of information regarding the 1923 campaign. Mississippi Department of Archives and History, Jackson, Miss.

84 CATCH THE VISION

Whitfield occasionally traveled by train, but most of the transportation was by automobile. Senator James O. Eastland, then a boy of eighteen, drove the automobile to many of the speaking engagements during the second primary. While making the trip to the Tupelo fair in a Model T Ford, Eastland and Whitfield were passed by Bilbo in his Apperson Jack Rabbit. Bilbo could pass Whitfield on the highway, but he was to have difficulty passing him at the polls. Eastland noted that Whitfield thoroughly enjoyed the campaign, loved to be with people, and was one of the best handshakers he ever saw. "He knew how to get to the people . . . knew how to get close to people," according to Eastland.[18]

Assured that he was receiving larger crowds than Bilbo, Whitfield was greatly encouraged. A thousand people gathered to hear him in Brookhaven—more than came for any other candidate. Approximately 1,500 people attended a Whitfield rally in Yazoo City.[19]

The Whitfield campaign operated on limited financial resources. He was determined to remain honest in all his actions and refused any support that would obligate him should the effort prove successful. Rocky Webster, campaign manager for Whitfield in Lafayette County, received a $75 check from a known Bilbo supporter. Whitfield told him to return the check along with other contributions that would tend to carry an obligation. At the conclusion of the campaign Whitfield paid a deficit by cashing a $10,000 life insurance policy.

Two slogans were used in Whitfield's campaign for Governor: "Win With Whitfield," which was displayed on many of the automobiles in the state; and "For a Better Mississippi," which was used in much of the newspaper publicity and appeared on the campaign placards which were attached to light poles, trees, and buildings.

---

[18] The 1923 Apperson was a car for the elite and designed to play its role in the elegant life. See Floyd Clymer, *Treasury of Early American Automobiles* (New York, 1950), p. 198.

[19] Columbus *Commercial Dispatch*, 15 July 1923; Yazoo City *Herald*, 21 August 1923.

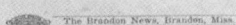

Campaign poster used in 1923

The campaign erupted into real fireworks when Whitfield went to Florence. On this July 4 the people of Florence wanted to go "all out" in honor of their former citizen who had become a candidate for Governor. In addition to a concert by the band, fireworks had been ordered especially for the occasion. Just before Whitfield was to speak, one of the local boys, through either ignorance or mischief, tossed a match or a cigarette into the box containing the fireworks. The people ran for cover as fireworks were sounding and shooting in all directions. Whitfield never moved from his seat on the platform and rose calmly to deliver the speech when the noise had subsided.

There were fireworks of a different kind which Whitfield had to face since no candidate for Governor could pass through the heat of a Mississippi political campaign without an occasional singeing. When he refused to debate Bilbo publicly, the former Governor remarked, "You Whitfield supporters have elected a standard bearer who is so weak that he cannot meet his opponent upon the stump." Bilbo insisted that he, with twelve years experience in public affairs, was much more qualified to be Governor than the "old man who has been up at the II&C learnin' the ladies how to crochet." He delighted in referring to Whitfield as "a good ole man." According to Mrs. Bilbo, her husband secretly admired Whitfield, but feared that if he were elected Governor the people would form circles around him, meaning he would be most confused stepping from the role of educator into the role of politician.[20]

One of the factors most favorable to Whitfield in the campaign was the active support of many women. Having received the right to vote in 1920, approximately 100,000 women had registered to vote in Mississippi in the election of 1923. The editor of the Clarksdale *Daily Register* spoke for most of the politicians when he said, "The woman vote is recognized by politicians throughout Mississippi as the deciding factor in the coming election."[21]

---

[20] Winona *Times*, 17 August 1923; Yazoo City *Herald*, 21 August 1923; Winona *Times*, 17 August 1923.
[21] Meridian *Star*, 26 August 1923; Clarksdale *Daily Register*, 16 July 1923.

Bilbo underestimated Whitfield, who as President of II&C for thirteen years had gained an obvious advantage with the female vote. The editor of the Vicksburg *Herald* claimed that Whitfield's popularity with the students "made him more women friends than merely those who were in college under him, and also many men friends who have been influenced by the good opinion of him by his former students." [22]

> As head of MSCW, Mr. Whitfield had attempted to make use of a rather remarkable device to unify the conflicting factions of his state. . . . Since the University of Mississippi at Oxford has always maintained a reputation for catering mainly to the delta people, and since the Agricultural and Mechanical College at Starkville is primarily designed to fill the needs of the inhabitants of the hill country, Mr. Whitfield conceived the idea of trying to minimize social strife in the state by creating common interests and sympathies among the women students of all classes who should attend MSCW. Towards this end, exclusive social organizations were never allowed; all students occupied similar quarters in dormitories; and all were required to wear simple uniforms of navy blue suits with black hats.[23]

The girls were obviously convinced that this same attitude could bring an end to factionalism in Mississippi.

Prior to his entrance into the campaign for Governor, Whitfield sent word to several former students asking them the question, "If I decide to run for governor, can you get three votes for me?" Immediately came the reply, "More than three!" In order to encourage support from all former students, each one received the following letter.

> For two reasons, I am addressing this letter in circular form to those who attended the MSCW during my presidency: First, because my message is the same. Second, because of the saving of expense.
> As you know, I am a candidate for the office of Governor. I have tried to conduct the cleanest campaign that was ever

---

[22] V. O. Key, Jr., *Southern Politics in State and Nation* (New York, 1949), p. 242; Vicksburg *Herald*, 10 June 1923.
[23] Clarence E. Cason, "The Mississippi Imbroglio," *Virginia Quarterly Review* 7(1931):237.

carried on in the state, and, I think I can say without the least exhibition of immodesty that it has been a successful campaign.

As it is doubtless known to most of you, political rivalry often makes men pursue what are known as "political methods" in an effort to advance the political interests of their friends. One of the favorite methods of trying to discredit the leading candidate in the eyes of the voters is, at what is supposed to be the psychological time, to put out propaganda to the effect that the leading candidate is fast losing his strength. Another method is for the friends of certain candidates to always name some other candidate as his leading opponent in order that the strength of his *leading* candidate may be underestimated, and an opponent is surer for the second primary that their candidate can defeat. I hope my friends will be on the lookout for such propaganda. If it is not now in circulation, it will be soon. Be prepared to denounce it as propaganda. I can say with perfect candor that I am stronger now before the people than at any other time.

Please speak and write letters to your friends in my interest. The battle is now on and I am trusting to my many friends to become active in my interest.[24]

In addition to this general letter, there were specific personal letters sent to former students; for example:

I appreciate more than I can express to you in a letter the sweet letter you wrote me. I did not intend to run, and I found it hard to get my own consent to make the race; I believed, under the conditions existing, that it was my duty to run.

My announcement has met with the most enthusiastic reception and I am anxious to take advantage of this favorable wave for me; now is the psychological time for my friends to serve. Will you not get as many of the Yazoo girls as you can, not only to speak to their relatives and friends about my candidacy, but to write to a number of their school friends to do the same.

Again, the girls of the county could help by getting up a club to do systematic work in my interest in Yazoo county and in the state generally.

Every one is saying what a strength the girls will be for me. Now, I feel that they are absolutely with me, yet if something is not done by them in an organized way for me in the various counties, I fear such will be noticed, and will cause somewhat of

---

[24] Copy in possession of Mrs. Charles F. Clark, Hendersonville, N.C.

a reaction against me. Will you not see Francis Blunt, your sister, Wilie Mae Williford, Ethel Bennett, and the others [to help] you do something in an organized way for me? [25]

Whitfield personally called on Mrs. Swep S. Taylor to request that she serve as the women's manager for the state. She gladly accepted the challenge and worked diligently in organizing the women in his behalf. There was some kind of Whitfield organization in every town where two or more MSCW alumnae lived. "I was president of the Jones County organization," stated Mrs. R. E. Mulloy. "We wrote letters, phoned friends over the state . . . put it over as big as love can do." The following resolution is typical of the work of the Whitfield Clubs.

> WHEREAS, the just pride of the womanhood and manhood of our state and its good name and fame abroad is suffering and has too long suffered by the immoral character of men we have elected Governors of Mississippi;
> AND WHEREAS, we should highly value and earnestly strive for the good opinion of mankind and maintain our own self for the good opinion of mankind and maintain our own self respect by electing a Chief Executor whose administration will respond to our highest ideals of good morals, good citizenship and honest Government;
> AND WHEREAS, a decent and honest Government is the only basis for loyalty and true patriotism;
> AND WHEREAS, the time has come when the moral character of the womanhood and manhood of the State must assert itself and resolve and decree that the pride and good name of Mississippi shall be redeemed and restored and her banner untarnished and unstained again unfurled among the banners of our proud Sister States;
> THEREFORE, Be it Resolved by the Whitfield Club of Women Voters of Lauderdale County that we know Hon. H. L. Whitfield, we know him as an individual and we know him as a public official. His private life has always been above reproach and his official record above any just criticism. He has discharged all of his official duties with credit to himself and to the satisfaction of the people of the State. He has given 24 years of service to the State, 13 of which he served as President of the

[25] Henry L. Whitfield to Miss Annie Ree Johnson, 5 July 1922, copy in possession of Mrs. Charles F. Clark, Hendersonville, N.C.

MSCW. The trying duties of his office as President of the College fully tested out the qualities of the man. In every trying situation he conducted himself with poise, and always carried a level head. The support which the people of Columbus and the army of young women in every part of the State who graduated under his administration who are now enthusiastically supporting him as a candidate for Governor is the very highest proof of his qualifications as a public official. We invite and will welcome cooperation of all good men and women to cooperate with us in electing Hon. H. L. Whitfield Governor of Mississippi.[26]

Practically every county in the state had at least one woman speaker in the interest of Whitfield. Former students introduced him on many occasions as he visited various communities of the state. "Wherever he went in 1923 he found his girls waiting and ready to help in any possible way they could to tell the voters that Mississippi needs could best be served by Mr. Whitfield," according to Mrs. Lillian Wigransky, a former student.[27]

An amusing episode which took place in Osyka illustrates the enthusiasm and boldness of the former students. One morning a former student received a package of Whitfield posters along with a request that they be distributed throughout the town. With help from a second former student, she soon placed the posters on light poles and in store windows. Upon entering the store of a staunch Bilbo supporter, one of the girls enticed the owner to the back for the purchase of five cents worth of tacks while the other placed a Whitfield poster in the window. Then the girls had great fun sitting outside watching the surprised and amused expressions on the faces of people as they passed by.

Bilbo fanned the zealous flame of the girls with certain unkind remarks about their former President. While speaking in Clay County, he referred to Whitfield as a fine man and promised to use him in the future as head of the old ladies home. In Hazlehurst, Bilbo said something derogatory about Whitfield only to have one of the II&C girls stand up and call him a liar. That terminated the meeting.

---

[26] Meridian *Star*, 6 July 1923.
[27] Jackson *Woman Voter*, 14 September 1923; Columbus *Commercial Dispatch*, 15 July 1923.

In addition to the Lee County Fair and the Neshoba County Fair, the Patron's Union in Newton County, about two miles north of Lake, was a popular place for the candidates. The Union, founded in 1883 by the Granges of Newton, Scott, Lauderdale, Neshoba, Jasper, Smith, Leake, and other adjoining counties, for the promotion of fraternal unity and educational, agricultural, and social advancement, was disbanded in the midthirties. During the 1923 election Whitfield spoke to thousands of people here. The II&C girls gathered under the tabernacle for a pep meeting. When the class president introduced their candidate, they sang songs and gave cheers. In Yazoo City the girls staged a political parade in support of Whitfield.[28] Wherever he went his girls would encourage him by singing,

> Here's to Mr. Whitfield, bless his heart, bless his heart.
> Here's to Mr. Whitfield, bless his heart.
> All the girls in blue
> Are every inch for you.
> Here's to Mr. Whitfield, bless his heart.

In order to illustrate the interest and activity of the II&C girls the following testimonies are included.

> Every girl that I knew was working for Mr. Whitfield in that campaign. All of the MSCW girls rallied to the cause. We wrote to friends, relatives, and acquaintances urging they support Mr. Whitfield.
>
> I handed out dodgers for him that hot summer.
>
> I ran my car in the '23 election and carried people to the polls to vote.
>
> I worked very hard before the election day and all day for him.
>
> I worked at the polls at Berea in Attala County for Mr. Whitfield and we carried the box for him.
>
> I personally stayed at one of the election polling places on the day of the election and worked for him.

Following the election, the Memphis *Commercial Appeal* printed a caricature of a car, loaded with women voters, running

---

[28] Yazoo City *Herald*, 13 July 1923.

over Bilbo. The caption read, "Who says a woman can't handle a car?" The editor of the Jackson *Daily News* reported, "The women have spoken by their ballots." A later article in the *Journal of Southern History* correctly concluded, "In Mississippi Henry L. Whitfield . . . was elected governor in 1923, largely through the efforts of alumnae of the college." [29]

In addition to the enthusiastic support of former students, a number of influential personalities joined with Whitfield forces for the battle with Bilbo. Harry Bryan, son-in-law of Chancellor Alfred Hume of the University of Mississippi, became campaign manager. Colonel Sydney McLaurin, prominent Brandon lawyer and brother of former Governor A. J. McLaurin, was a great influencing factor in Whitfield's decision to enter the race and one of his most fervent supporters. Sennett (Mike) Conner endorsed Whitfield in the second primary. John Sharp Williams stated publicly that he would vote for Whitfield. Judge Percy Bell sent a telegram to Whitfield stating, "In furtherance of my fight for decency in Mississippi's political life, I shall support you against Bilbo whom I consider a menace to the state." Many other prominent personalities including Mississippi College President, Dr. J. W. Provine, Senator H. D. Stephens, and former Governor Earl Brewer, worked for Whitfield.[30]

Another tremendously important factor in the success of Whitfield was the state newspapers, eighty percent of which supported him in the second primary. The support of these newspapers enabled Whitfield to keep the issues of the campaign clearly before the people; the planks in his platform expressed the major issues. Even with strong newspaper support, Whitfield was forced to endure the onslaught of much stinging criticism from those newspapers which opposed him. The Yazoo *Sentinel*, in urging support for Bilbo, spoke of Whitfield as "an

[29] Memphis *Commercial Appeal*, 30 August 1923; Jackson *Daily News*, 30 August 1923; Anne Firor Scott, "After Suffrage: Southern Women in the Twenties," *The Journal of Southern History* 30 (1964): 315.
[30] Grenada *Sentinel*, 17 August 1923; Columbus *Commercial Dispatch*, 29 July 1923; Harry Bryan Scrapbook, 5; Marion *County Progress*, 23 August 1923; Winona *Times*, 24 August 1923.

untried entity in statecraft. Many of his supporters admit that he is a man of mediocre ability." The editor of the McComb *Enterprise* said that "he has never so far as we have been able to learn ever advocated or formulated a thought or a thing that would be for the betterment of Mississippi." The Poplarville *Free Press* was not as fierce in opposing Whitfield since no question was raised regarding the morality of the candidate, though it did pose questions about his executive ability.[31]

The Ripley *Southern Sentinel* strongly supported Bilbo and opposed Whitfield for advocating an open door to outside capital. "Bilbo is able. He is patriotic," said the editor, and "he wants to make Mississippi a great governor. He will not turn the state over to the corporations for private plunder." The Senatobia *Democrat* opposed Whitfield by calling him a high tax man. He sought to refute this attack by calling attention to his economical operation of II&C, indicating that he could give the state more for the present tax dollar without making the tax load heavier.[32]

Whitfield did not pass through the heat of the campaign without making blunders, and there were times when he gave evidence of a lack of knowledge in the arena of state politics. For example, while speaking in Grenada he questioned the importance of platforms by saying that he could not conceive of L. Q. C. Lamar or James Z. George having a platform. In doing this he failed to distinguish between the period in which they lived and his own. In the days of Lamar and George the Democrats of the state met every election year and adopted a platform of party principles for the candidate to stand on. In the later period the party convention was fixed by law only once in four years, and that during a presidential election. Therefore it was fitting that the people be informed regarding how the candidate stood on certain issues.[33]

---

[31] Jackson *Daily Clarion-Ledger*, 19 August 1923; Yazoo *Sentinel*, 13 August 1923; McComb *Enterprise*, 30 August 1923; Poplarville *Free Press*, 23 August 1923.
[32] Poplarville *Free Press*, 30 August 1923; Grenada *Sentinel*, 29 June 1923; Aberdeen *Weekly*, 15 June 1923.
[33] Grenada *Sentinel*, 3 August 1923.

94 CATCH THE VISION

When the votes were counted, Whitfield emerged the victor by a vote of 134,715 to 118,143. The map of Mississippi below indicates the counties which were carried by Whitfield.[34]

As one looks at the election returns objectively there are two obvious factors to be considered which greatly aided Whitfield. Bilbo was unable to make a good showing in influential Hinds County, where he was soundly defeated by over 3,000 votes. Another important feature of the election results was that Bilbo did not have the necessary strength in the Delta. The added returns of the eleven Delta counties consisting of Bolivar, Coahoma, Humphreys, Issaquena, Leflore, Quitman, Sharkey, Sunflower, Tallahatchie, Tunica, and Washington show that Whitfield carried the area by more than 8,000 votes.[35]

In addition to the favorable factors for Whitfield which were cited in the discussion of the campaign, there were other matters which contributed to his election. One of these was the growing sentiment of anti-Vardamanism in the state. "Vardaman's successor in the esteem of the underprivileged whites of Mississippi was Theodore G. Bilbo." The second primary was billed as a battle between the forces of Vardamanism, represented by Bilbo, and the forces of enlightened democracy, represented by Whitfield. Anti-Vardaman, anti-Bilbo, and anti-Russell factions gained control of the Democratic state convention in June 1920. To many Mississippians, who considered him a blatant demagogue and the father of factionalism, Bilbo represented an ugly phase of politics.[36]

Many looked upon the Whitfield campaign as an effort to redeem Mississippi from the demagogic influences of Vardaman and Bilbo. The Whitfield vote signaled a victory in this effort.

---

[34] *Biennial Report of the Secretary of State, 1921–1923*, p. 152.

[35] All statistics related to the election are taken from the *Biennial Report of the Secretary of State, 1921–1923*, p. 152; for an excellent treatment of Bilbo's problems with the Delta, see William D. McCain, "Theodore Gilmore Bilbo and the Mississippi Delta," *The Journal of Mississippi History* 21 (1969): 1–27.

[36] For excellent background material to the 1923 election, see Albert D. Kirwan, *Revolt of the Rednecks, Mississippi Politics, 1876–1925* (New York, 1951); Francis B. Simkins, *A History of the South*, p. 543; Greenville *Daily Democrat-Times*, 16 August 1923; Columbus *Commercial Dispatch*, 20 June 1923; Yazoo City *County News*, 20 August 1923.

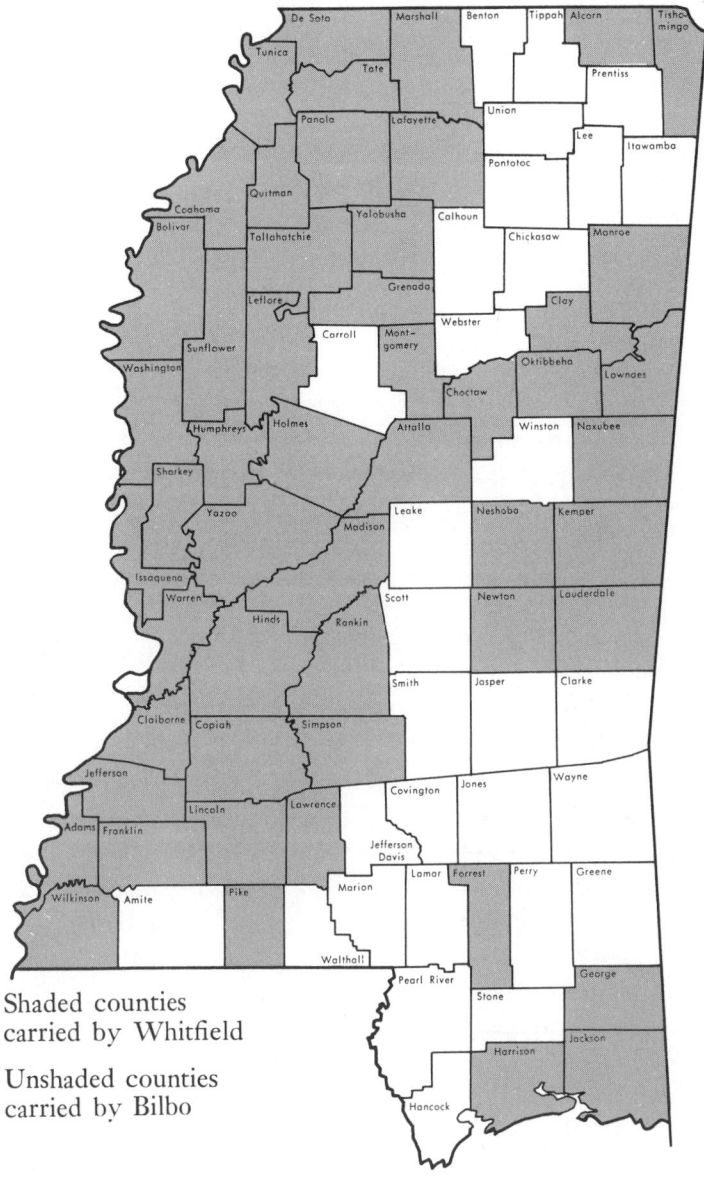

Shaded counties carried by Whitfield

Unshaded counties carried by Bilbo

When Henry L. Whitfield was elected Governor in 1924 [*sic*] the long fight appeared to be won. Whitfield typified the State's best traditions. By profession an educator . . . he had developed qualities of statemanship which promised to make him a servant of his state as dependable if not as brilliant as were L. Q. C. Lamar and John Sharp Williams.[37]

The editor of the Grenada *Sentinel* said that "the work of redemption which we have stood for and for which the *Sentinel* has striven for in past elections . . . should be completed by the nomination of Whitfield. . . ."[38]

In connection with the anti-Bilbo sentiment, the famous Birkhead affair must be considered. In 1922 Miss Frances Birkhead, former secretary to Governor Lee Russell, filed a $100,000 suit against him in federal court, charging that he had seduced her while promising marriage when a divorce could be arranged. Bilbo did not appear in court to testify, on the grounds that he had been Russell's attorney, thus obtaining confidential information which could not be disclosed. He was ultimately found in contempt of court and sentenced to ten days in the Oxford jail.[39]

The enemies of Bilbo were convinced that he had arranged the entire affair in order to publicly discredit Russell, which would leave him sole heir to this political faction. A person with intimate knowledge of the Birkhead affair stated that Bilbo planted the woman in Russell's office and paid her with money received from certain insurance companies which were suffering at the hands of Russell. The Bilbo faction claimed that he "was sent to jail because he would not violate a professional confidence and tell all he knew about the social affair of another person."[40]

Bilbo served his term in jail, although the warden put the place on a hotel basis for him. He was given a comfortable bedroom downstairs with neither bars nor locked doors, where he was

---

[37] "Why Mississippi Chose A Demagogue," *The Outlook* 147 (1927): 3–4.
[38] Grenada *Sentinel*, 17 August 1923.
[39] Kirwan, *Revolt of the Rednecks*, pp. 297, 298.
[40] Larry Thomas Balsamo, "Theodore G. Bilbo and Mississippi Politics, 1877–1932" (Ph.D dissertation, University of Missouri, 1967), p. 142; A. B. Friend, *Mississippi's Senior United States Senator* (n.p., 1946), p. 7.

served delicious meals and given the opportunity of receiving visitors day and night. Judge T. H. McElroy of Oxford, departing from a visit with Bilbo, remarked, "Governor, if I ever have to go to jail, I want this arrangement." While in jail, Bilbo claimed to have had a vision of overwhelming election returns, inaugural parades, and four years in the Governor's Mansion. "Refreshed by ten days of cloistered rest, from the steps of the jail The Man announced his candidacy for the office of governor, each of the ten planks in his platform representing one day in jail." Russell was acquitted, but the scandal was a real boost to Whitfield.[41]

Prior to the election State Senator Jeff Bell went to Birmingham to visit with Vardaman. Upon his return he declared that Vardaman refused to recognize Bilbo as either a personal friend or political ally. He also reported Vardaman as saying that Whitfield should be elected Governor. This episode was generally accepted to be true since Bilbo did not question it or make public issue of it.[42]

In addition to the above factors which worked to Whitfield's advantage in the election, there were other matters to be considered. One of these was that Whitfield was a person of great personal popularity and appeal. Also he was recognized as a diligent campaigner. W. E. McIntyre, Sr., campaign manager for Mike Conner, was impressed with the campaign ability of Whitfield. Whitfield's position was strengthened because he so easily made friends all his life and never forgot them.[43]

Following the election Whitfield issued a statement to the people of Mississippi.

> I appreciate more than I will ever be able to express in any way the confidence the majority of the voters of the state have manifested in making me the Democratic nominee for governor.

---

[41] Reinhard H. Luthin, *American Demagogues in the Twentieth Century* (Gloucester, 1959), p. 55; Jackson *Daily News*, 18 April 1923; A. Wigfall Green, *The Man Bilbo* (Baton Rouge, 1963), p. 69.
[42] Kirwan, *Revolt of the Rednecks*, p. 305.
[43] Pearl V. Guyton, *Our Mississippi* (Austin, 1959), p. 230.

98 CATCH THE VISION

The responsibility that this nomination imposes upon me will be hard to discharge but it is my intention to do my best to show by my acts that this confidence has not been misplaced. We face a grave crisis in our economic and financial affairs. I will need the support of all good men and women in the solution of all the complex problems that confront us.

It will be my earnest desire to be governor of all the people. I have but the kindest feelings for those who preferred my distinguished opponents for this office. They certainly had a right to vote for the man they thought best prepared for the position.

It is my purpose to stand for every thing that is constructive, economical and decent for the state, and I call on all good men and women to forget the differences, bickerings and divisions of the past and to join with me in an effort to make Mississippi a prosperous and happy state.

I shall go into office unpledged and I will be in a position at all times to decide for what I believe is best for the state.

Again thanking the people of the state for this opportunity for service. . . .[44]

"His election was unusual, as it had been customary for a politician of some years' experience in both houses of the legislature to be the chosen leader of the people."[45]

Rather than take life easy between election and inauguration, Whitfield maintained a busy schedule. He and his family did visit the Gulf Coast for a period of relaxation, but much of this time was devoted to a study of the needs of this area of the state, including meetings with the leaders of the fish and oyster industry. The Governor-elect made himself available for numerous speaking engagements, addressing Mississippi College students, whom he challenged to catch a vision of the greatness of their country and prepare themselves to meet their God-given obligations; the Louisiana and Mississippi Kiwanians in Baton Rouge, where he also played golf with the Governor of Louisiana; the Federated Clubs of Mississippi; and the Parent-Teacher Association of Columbus. Cowan Wall, one of the boys from

---

[44] Jackson *Daily News*, 5 September 1923.
[45] Charles S. Sydnor and Claude Bennett, *Mississippi History* (New York, 1930), pp. 351–52.

the Masonic orphanage, recalls with tearful eyes and loving appreciation that Whitfield accompanied him to Meridian during this time and helped him obtain a job.[46]

Whitfield was honored by the student body of MSCW. "No one else could have ever brought forth the unbounded enthusiasm from the student body as did Mr. Whitfield when he entered the College Chapel." All the girls rose, saying, "Here's to Mr. Whitfield, bless his heart, bless his heart." Following his speech he was given a tuxedo by the student body and a new set of golf clubs by the faculty, who desired that he be dubbed the "Greatest Golfing Governor." The Christmas holidays were spent working on the inaugural address in the mornings and playing golf in the afternoons.[47]

Following the Christmas holidays, Whitfield went to Jackson, where he secured a small room in the Royal Hotel at the rate of $1.50 per day. He lived there until the Governor's Mansion was vacated. When he came from his room in inaugural dress, none of the tags had been removed; obviously Mrs. Whitfield was not present, which was the only sad note of the day. She was ill and unable to make the trip. Even though he agreed to wear the long-tailed coat, Whitfield insisted he would not wear the "fool high hat." While he was delivering the inaugural address, his bald head became cold, forcing him to request a soft hat.[48]

An inaugural parade preceded Whitfield's induction into office. The day was clear and bright with an early morning temperature near freezing. The large inaugural parade began promptly at eleven o'clock and was nearly one hour passing a given point. Customarily the incoming and outgoing Governors rode in the same carriage or automobile, but this time Governor

[46] Jackson *Daily News*, 16 September 1923; 10 September 1923; 20 September 1923; 1 November 1923; Columbus *Commercial Dispatch*, 14 October 1923.
[47] Mississippi State College for Women *Spectator*, 15 December 1923; Columbus *Commercial Dispatch*, 26 December 1923.
[48] Dennis Murphree Memoirs, chap. 33 in possession of Mrs. Mary Frances Murphree Ford, Jackson, Miss.; Meridian *Star*, 22 January 1924; Dennis Murphree Memoirs, chap. 33; the content of the inaugural address is discussed in my Chapter IV, which deals with Whitfield's legislative program.

and Mrs. Lee Russell chose to occupy a separate car. Jackson police served as escort with the A. and M. Cadet Band serving as the official band for the occasion. There were approximately 5,000 people in the line of march headed by Adjutant General Erie C. Scales, Grand Marshal. Some of the participants were Chief Justice Sydney Smith, the Joint Inaugural Committee, National Guard officers, Lieutenant Governor and Mrs. Dennis Murphree, the Mississippi Legislature, and all state officers.[49]

When Whitfield took the oath of office, administered by Chief Justice Sydney M. Smith, his hand rested on Matthew 20:26–27, "Whosoever will be great among you, let him be your minister; and whosoever will be chief among you, let him be your servant." The oath of office was preceded by a prayer led by the Reverend W. A. Hewitt, pastor of Jackson's First Baptist Church. There was an inaugural ball at the City Auditorium, but the new Governor did not attend.[50]

The inauguration of Henry Whitfield marked the beginning of a new era in politics and public life in the state. The editor of the Memphis *Commercial Appeal* spoke the sentiments of Whitfield's supporters when he said,

> Mr. Whitfield is a man of ability, unassailable integrity, and of high ideals. We hope, and have every reason to believe, that not only will he administer the affairs of his office wisely and economically, but that he will bridge the chasm between the warring factions of the Democratic party, put an end to strife, and restore to Mississippi the glory that is rightfully hers.[51]

The editor of the Jackson *Daily News* described the new spirit which was wrought by the Whitfield administration when he said, "It marked the end of the bitter factionalism, rampant radicalism, cheap demagogy, damnable corruption, and the ugly trial of scandal and indecency with which the state had so long been cursed." [52]

---

[49] Unless otherwise noted, the description of the inaugural parade and ceremonies are taken from Jackson *Daily News,* 22 January 1924.
[50] Meridian *Star,* 11 January 1924.
[51] Memphis *Commercial Appeal,* 31 August 1923.
[52] Jackson *Daily News,* 18 March 1927.

The Governor was determined to bring an honest administration to the state. "There was no man [who] ever questioned his honesty, and no man [who] ever administered the office in finer devotion to the interests of the people."[53] H. D. (Rocky) Webster, Whitfield's campaign manager for Lafayette County, was asked what he received for his efforts. He responded by saying, "Only the privilege of electing a good Governor—no one profited dishonestly from his administration." Purser Hewitt, editor of the Jackson *Clarion-Ledger*, stated that Whitfield "did not take graft, in fact, he did not know how." "He could have sold out and been a millionaire," according to one of his secretaries, but "you could not buy Whitfield, he was not for sale at any price."

Governor Whitfield abided by his campaign promise that he had pledged no patronage. Consequently, when office seekers approached him they were treated in a nonpartisan manner.[54] Henry Boswell, head of the Sanitarium, presented his resignation only to hear the Governor say, "Go on back and I will tell you when I want your resignation." The director of the state mental institution had a similar experience. A lady who worked in the tax commission under the Russell administration feared the loss of her job. Whitfield told her that he would forget that she did not vote for him, for he was seeking qualified people. She did not lose her job. Macey Dinkins had served as secretary to Lee Russell, and his wife had served as secretary to James K. Vardaman; he was retained as secretary to Whitfield.

Determined to give his personal attention to the institutions and problems of the state, Whitfield was a very busy Governor. He attended all meetings of the eleemosynary governing boards in order to keep in close touch with all needs. When the board of trustees of the South Mississippi Charity Hospital met, he was there. He personally toured the educational centers of the state in order to study the situation of each. When the trustees of higher institutions were in session, he was present. He also at-

[53] Jackson *Baptist Record*, 24 March 1923.
[54] Jackson *Daily News*, 7 December 1923.

tended the trustee meetings of other institutions such as Beauvoir and the Columbia Training School. The Governor could be seen studying the levee lines of the Mississippi River in Vicksburg and Greenville, visiting the Piney Woods School, and meeting with the Oyster Commission on the coast. When there were specific needs, such as a request for the commutation of death sentences, he would conduct a personal investigation on the scene. He was never inclined toward laziness.[55]

In addition to attending various board and trustee meetings, Governor Whitfield maintained a very busy speaking schedule. Some of his speaking engagements included the Mississippi Federation of Woman's Clubs, Annual Conference of Home Demonstration Workers in Birmingham, Memphis MSCW Alumnae Association, radio station WMC in Memphis, Florence High School, United States Veteran's Hospital in Gulfport, Mississippi Press Association meeting in Meridian, Baylor College in Texas, Mississippi A. and M. College, Annual Convention of American Legion, Confederate Veterans, Hi-Y Clubs of Simpson County, Mississippi College Alumni Banquet, Louisiana State Normal College, Chautauqua meeting in Little Rock, annual convention of the Mississippi Federation of Labor and the Democratic National Convention in New York.

Because of his background, the Governor always maintained a vital interest in education. "Profound as was the Governor's interest in the improvement of the economic, industrial, and social conditions of his people, it was not his deepest passion. Education lay closer to his heart than anything else." When asked where the best energies of the state were being applied, he responded with "the education of our people." In addition to his legislative program affecting education as discussed in chapter four, he did two things to strengthen the educational framework of Mississippi. First, he sought every opportunity to challenge and encourage the teachers. This was accomplished in three ways—personal correspondence, personal addresses, and appro-

---

[55] Jackson *Daily News*, 8 April 1925; 18 April 1924; 27 March 1926; 24 November 1925; 12 April 1926; 20 April 1926; 22 April 1926; 9 September 1925; Jackson *Daily Clarion-Ledger*, 18 July 1924.

Governor Whitfield presenting the Commercial Dispatch Cup for outstanding citizenship to Mr. Ed Kykendall

104 CATCH THE VISION

priately written articles. An example of personal correspondence can be seen in the following excerpt: "[I] . . . am glad to know that you have secured a teacher who will be in sympathy with the general idea of having the work of colleges bear directly on the concrete problems of the state." [56]

An example of Whitfield's use of the public address can be seen in his appearance before the faculty and students of the State Normal School. He spoke of "rights" and "duties," while noting that the time had come when new emphasis should be placed on "duties." "Selfishness demands 'rights,'" stated the Governor, "but 'duties' look to a higher aim—that of building character, upon which the stability of the government depends." [57]

An example of an article can be observed in Whitfield's use of the *Mississippi Educational Advance*. Writing to the teachers, he said, "Our own State is about to go through a complete industrial revolution with its accompanying upheaval in its political and general social life." Consequently, he challenged every teacher in the state to "have interest and ability sufficient to visualize this new State in the making, and carry the boys and girls up to the heights to see what they will have to do if they compete successfully. . . ." The Governor reminded the teachers that "knowledge, skill, character, patriotism, education of body, mind and soul, of head, heart and hand, all needed today, will be more indispensable tomorrow." [58]

The second thing which Whitfield did to strengthen the educational system of Mississippi was to commission a number of educational specialists to make a study of the "curriculum methods of teaching in all departments of the public school system, including the colleges and University, for the purpose of determining whether improvements could be made in the

---

[56] M. V. O'Shea, *A State Educational System At Work* (Jackson, 1927), p. v; Jackson *Daily News*, 11 December 1925; H. L. Whitfield to J. C. Fant, 15 January 1926, located in H. L. Whitfield correspondence, John Clayton Fant Memorial Library, Mississippi State College for Women.
[57] Jackson *Daily News*, 18 June 1924.
[58] Henry L. Whitfield, "A Message From Governor Whitfield," *The Mississippi Educational Advance* 15 (1924): 8, 46.

educational work of the state." The Governor was greatly interested in this study and every night he called the investigators together at the Governor's Mansion for intense discussions. "The Governor was always the dominating force in these free-for-all tournaments." Whitfield died before he could make use of this investigating report.[59]

Governor Whitfield wanted his people to know Mississippi, believing this would make them more active in the affairs of the state. "After 25 years in public life in Mississippi," the Governor remarked, "I am convinced that the most pressing need of this State is a more active, intelligent, and continuous interest in public affairs on the part of the thinking people of Mississippi." In order to accomplish this, he distributed his small book, *Know Mississippi*, throughout the state.

In addition to challenging the people to know Mississippi, Whitfield also wanted them to buy in Mississippi. He issued a statement to promote this objective.

> We want now to put on a campaign for the buying of Mississippi products. We want to see Mississippi canned goods and other products on the shelves of the merchants. If the merchants sell Mississippi-made goods, the people will buy them. We are now producing products of every kind in the state. These should be sold inside the state, and the surplus then sold outside the state. We have products of every kind in an available form and we will expect the loyal people of Mississippi to give Mississippi products the preference in their buying. Buy Mississippi products, use Mississippi products and keep our money at home. The home merchant pays the taxes and helps to make the community and state progressive, so does the home manufacturer. So we will expect the loyal Mississippians to buy at home and use Mississippi products.[60]

Added to his pet themes of "Know Mississippi" and "Buy in Mississippi" was the Governor's appeal to "Create Opportunities in Mississippi." He had no patience with the young people who left the state after accepting the educational opportunities which were offered. Whitfield exclaimed, "They say there are no op-

---

[59] O'Shea, *A State Educational System*, pp. 3, iv.
[60] Jackson *Daily Clarion-Ledger*, 2 June 1925.

106 CATCH THE VISION

portunities here, but that is why they are educated, to make those opportunities and to grasp those before them." [61]

During his tenure as Governor, religion continued to play a prominent role in the life of Henry Whitfield. He served as deacon in the First Baptist Church of Jackson, welcomed the opportunity to teach the Bible, spoke at evangelistic rallies, and occupied the pulpit in churches of all denominations. His was a familiar face at the morning prayer services in the Department of Education. He aided in the promotion of the Seventy-Five Million Campaign, which was an effort to lift the Southern Baptist Convention out of a pressing financial position. When the congregation of the First Baptist Church in Jackson sought to raise $120,000 for the building fund, he was present to shoulder his share of the responsibility.[62]

The Governor supported the work of various evangelists. Among these was a well-known lay-evangelist named Howard Williams. Whitfield's attitude toward this man and his work can be seen in the following letter, which he wrote to Williams.

> I have watched with great pleasure your Evangelistic work since you first began it. I have been in two of your meetings and want to say that you have my earnest support in the great work which you are doing.
> You are preaching righteousness in Mississippi and Mississippi needs more righteousness at this time. We have a great state, one of great possibilities. We have a fine-fibred people, but our people must recognize God and learn to obey Him.
> May God bless you in your great work to make Mississippi a greater and cleaner state.[63]

When Evangelist Billy Sunday came to Jackson, the Governor was at the head of the welcoming party. He attended the services regularly and took his seat on the platform near Sunday.[64]

Henry Whitfield brought to the governor's office a new attitude toward race relations, which prompted the *New Outlook* to call him the "Apostle of Racial Good Will."

---

[61] Jackson *Daily News*, 12 February 1924.
[62] Ibid., 18 March 1927; 24 January 1926; 31 July 1926; Jackson *Daily Clarion-Ledger*, 13 July 1924; Jackson *Daily News*, 27 April 1924; 6 May 1924.
[63] Jackson *Daily News*, 23 July 1924.
[64] Ibid., 28 December 1924.

When Henry L. Whitfield became Governor of Mississippi in January, the event marked the dawn of a new era in race relations in a commonwealth where the blacks outnumber the whites. Whitfieldism is the antithesis of Vardamanism. Instead of fomenting racial friction by making rabid anti-Nego speeches, Governor Whitfield and his followers are bending their efforts toward unifying the two races for their common good.[65]

He viewed the Negro as a human being who was entitled to a square deal of which he had been deprived. He set forth his position by saying,

> While maintaining absolutely inviolate separate racial integrity, how may the two races live side by side and promote a better feeling of inter-racial cooperation and good will and thus make all our citizens more prosperous, more contented and more conscious of the obligations to the state?[66]

The Negro had suffered at the hands of those who advocated white supremacy. Senator James Z. George spoke the mind of many politicians when he said, "White predominance must be secured in order that good government may be maintained." Former Governor Theodore Bilbo's attitude toward the "nigger," as he called him, had greatly affected the racial climate in the state. The Negro had been largely disfranchised in 1890. In that year a constitutional convention was called for the purpose of finding a "legal method" whereby the political supremacy of the white race could be maintained. The disfranchisement was accomplished under the new constitution by requiring voters to give a reasonable interpretation of any section of the constitution, the payment of a poll tax for two years preceding an election in order to vote, and by disfranchising those convicted of enumerated crimes.[67]

The racial climate was made even more stormy by the activity

---

[65] Lester A. Walton, "Whitfield—Apostle of Racial Good Will," *New Outlook* 136 (1924): 589.
[66] Whitfield, *Know Mississippi*, p. 83.
[67] James P. Coleman, "The Mississippi Constitution of 1890 and the Final Decade of the Nineteenth Century," *A History of Mississippi*, ed. Richard Aubrey McLemore, 2 vols. (Hattiesburg, 1973) 2: 9, 14; Kirwan, *Revolt of the Rednecks*, pp. 65-71.

108 CATCH THE VISION

of the Ku Klux Klan. "By the summer of 1921, almost a hundred thousand klansmen had paid their money and stepped across the mystic threshold to take their chances in the invisible empire." By 1925 between four and five million Americans had enrolled in the Klan. One of the major thrusts of the Klan was denouncing the Negro. No study has been made on the Klan activity in Mississippi between 1920 and 1930; however, one may assume that the state did not escape the Klan influence.[68]

Desiring to implement a better racial climate in Mississippi, Governor Whitfield took definite steps. He made it clear that he would be the Governor of all the people, including the Negroes. Because he was vitally concerned that thousands of Negroes were leaving the farms of Mississippi and going to the industrial centers of the North and Middle West, the Governor stated emphatically that any plan for the future economic life of Mississippi which did not include the Negro would be doomed to failure. He desired to improve the working and living conditions of the Negro, look after his health, and give him a square deal in business relations and the courts.[69]

Whitfield wanted the Negro treated fairly in matters of law. For example, James Wallace, a Negro youth in Leflore County, was under sentence to hang. The Governor commuted the sentence to life imprisonment. Sam H. Long, prominent Tupelo attorney, called on the Governor to commute the death sentence of a seventeen-year-old Negro youth. Attorney Long told him that it would not be either popular or politically advantageous to do this. Whitfield replied that he was not concerned with the consequences as he instructed his secretary to write up a commutation of the sentence to life imprisonment.[70]

The Governor abhorred mob violence and called for the recognition of the supremacy of the law and the equality of every man before the bar of justice. He urged all law-enforcing officials

---

[68] David M. Chalmers, *Hooded Americanism: The First Century of the Ku Klux Klan 1865–1965* (New York, 1965), p. 33; Simkins, *A History of the South*, p. 559.
[69] Mississippi *House Journal* (1924), pp. 219–20.
[70] Jackson *Daily News*, 29 November 1925, 1.

to use every means possible to prevent lynchings, thus eliminating a major cause of racial strife and ill feeling. Prosperity for both races and protection of their lives and property were the ultimate goals of the Governor. Following the lynching of a Negro near New Albany, he said, "This crime against the law is shocking to every sense of respect for law and Christianity." To Whitfield the rape of a woman was a horrible crime, but the rape of the law by an angry and infuriated mob was also a horrible crime.[71]

Another thing which Whitfield did to promote better racial relations was to give his time in speaking to various Negro groups. He spoke to the Negro Baptist Convention, the Utica Normal and Industrial Institute, and the Negro college in Okolona. The Governor also welcomed Negroes to visit in his office. On one occasion he received a letter from Negroes in New York requesting an audience. They were received graciously and the Governor heard their protest concerning a certain lynching. When they had finished, he said, "This is the first time we have had Negroes to protest the lynching of a white man." The delegation had assumed that only Negroes were lynched in Mississippi. The Governor took another significant step on behalf of the Negro by appointing T. G. Ewing, a Negro lawyer of Vicksburg, Notary Public.[72]

Whitfield's attitude and action in the area of race relations brought criticism. Some called him a "nigger lover." The Mississippi *Free Lance*, Bilbo's newspaper, stated that

> Governor Whitfield who has all along shown a dear fondness for Mississippi's Ethiopian products, has appointed a "coal black buck" as Notary Public, to serve the good people in the classic and aristocratic old southern city . . . of Vicksburg.[73]

There were others who praised the Governor for his stand. The editor of the Jackson *Daily News* commented, "We all know . . . that we have not been giving the negro a square deal,

[71] Mississippi *House Journal* (1924), p. 220; Jackson *Daily News*, 21 September 1925.
[72] Jackson *Daily News*, 21 July 1924; 2 February 1925; 6 May 1924.
[73] Jackson *Free Lance*, 8 May 1924.

110 CATCH THE VISION

and it is gratifying to know that we have a Governor endowed with the courage to speak right out and tell the truth about it." [74]

Whitfield's disposition in the racial area resulted in certain definite responses. According to the Jackson *Daily News*, the Negro exodus stopped and many blacks who left Mississippi returned. Scores of Negroes who had joined the northern exodus several years earlier could be seen in the state. Another significant change was the noticeable advance in appropriations for the fiscal year 1925–26 in the departments of vocational agriculture in Negro schools. A vitally important response in the Governor's effort to create an improved racial climate was the personal encouragement which the Negro community felt. This statement is verified by a letter sent to the Governor by the Committee of One Hundred, an organization designed to improve the welfare of the Negro race.[75]

> We are the executive officers of The Committee of One Hundred, an organization of leaders of the negro race from every county and eighteen from the state at large—working for the general improvement of the condition of the colored people and for the welfare of Mississippi. Along with other citizens we have read with much interest your recent inaugural address; and have taken special notice of that part of the message which concerns our group so vitally on "Interracial Relations." It is part of the message about which we would like to write you.
>
> Your discussion of this much mooted question is indeed broad, sympathetic and statesman-like. It is a substantial contribution in the way of encouragement to the untiring efforts of the leaders to develop a better and more useful citizenship among our people. Certainly when the highest official of the commonwealth speaks thus, the negro has another big reason for not losing faith in Mississippi.[76]

This letter indicates that the Negro community was obviously

---

[74] Jackson *Daily News*, 23 January 1924.
[75] Ibid., 1 September 1925; Charles H. Wilson, *Education For Negroes in Mississippi Since 1910* (Boston, 1947), p. 315.
[76] J. E. Johnson to Henry L. Whitfield, printed in the Jackson *Daily News*, 29 January 1924.

most pleased by the attitude of the Governor toward race relations.

Three very important events in which Whitfield participated carried him beyond the borders of Mississippi. The first of these was a trip to Wisconsin. In the fall of 1924 a significant interest in the dairying industry had developed. In order to learn more about this industry and how it could be improved in Mississippi, Governor Whitfield conducted a delegation of farmers, bankers, and businessmen to Wisconsin for a two-week study of the dairy industry in that state. The two-week inspection trip covered twelve counties with visits to numerous farms, cheese plants, and creameries. The delegation sought to obtain information which could be brought back and shared with Mississippi farmers, dairymen, and county agents.[77]

The Wisconsin trip proved most successful because the information which was returned to Mississippi resulted in an increased interest in the dairy industry and an increase in the production of milk in several counties. In Clay County negotiations with Swift and Company resulted in the acquisition of an additional processing plant in West Point. Two other plants were located in neighboring towns.[78]

In the fall of 1925 Governor Whitfield called for a special Southwide Conference to be held in Birmingham, Ala., October 28 and 29. The purpose of the conference was to discuss a variety of subjects related to the South with special emphasis on federal aid.

> On its program was some of the best talent ever assembled in a meeting of this character. One of the prominent speakers, Dr. Frederick L. Hoffman, an internationally noted statistical consultant of the Prudential Insurance Company of America, discussed at length the subject of Southern Progress and Welfare. Dr. Hoffman's address was no less illuminating than the addresses of J. E. LePrince, senior Sanitary engineer of the U. S.

[77] Account of the Wisconsin trip written by J. T. Ruble of West Point is in possession of The Mississippi Department of Archives and History; Jackson *Daily News*, 28 September 1924.
[78] Ibid.

Health Department, Elwood Meade, U. S. Commissioner of Reclamation, Copely Amory, U. S. Special expert on Reclamation economics, E. E. Blake, chairman of the Oklahoma Irrigation Drainage and Reclamation Commission and Honorable Hugh MacRae, noted for his extensive work on colonization.[79]

Governor Whitfield was the keynote speaker for the opening session of the conference. He noted that the South had not received its rightful share of the national resources and wanted and needed additional federal aid. He cited some of the vast projects which the national government had undertaken in the West, while questioning why the South had not received comparable attention and aid. The Governor continued by remarking,

> I regret to know that there has arisen some objection in the east to the government's participation in some of these great national projects. I would remind our neighbors of the east that the national government has expended untold millions in the building of harbors for the New England and Middle Atlantic states and that this very governmental help has made it possible for these eastern seaports to become the outlets for vast commerce of the country. This commerce has brought countless wealth to these states. I feel sure that when our friends in the east remember these government benefits which they have received, they will withdraw any opposition which they may have to the national government assisting the South in the solution of her problems which solution will make for the progress and prosperity and happiness of the whole country.[80]

The Southwide Conference was attended by seven governors, several congressmen, and special delegations from the Southern states. The conference resulted in the appointment of a special committee, of which Whitfield was a member, to lay plans for a permanent Southern organization. The Southern Governors' Conference, as it is known today, dates its beginning from 1934, but it is probable that at the 1925 meeting the idea of a permanent Southern organization was conceived.[81]

---

[79] "South Wide Conference Termed Great Success," *The Mississippi Developer* 1 (1925): 2.
[80] Jackson *Daily News*, 28 October 1925.
[81] *The Mississippi Developer* 1 (1925): 2.

Governor of Mississippi 113

In addition to the Southern conference, Whitfield exerted his influence beyond Mississippi by calling a regional Cotton Conference in 1926. The meeting, convened in Memphis, was precipitated by the great crisis that threatened to bankrupt the Southern cotton grower in 1926, when cotton prices decreased below prewar levels because of overproduction. Mississippi's chief executive summoned governors of the cotton-growing states to gather for the purpose of working out a plan to relieve the farmer and avert a financial panic. George Brown Tindall gives an excellent brief account of this important conference and the results.[82]

> The continuing slide of cotton prices . . . brought another cotton convention. Governor H. L. Whitfield of Mississippi called the meeting at Memphis in October, 1926, with the anticipation that "a time of great necessity" had brought the psychological situation "that causes the people to quit the old systems of business and adopt new ones." The new system, it transpired, was another holding effort—but the boldest yet—with cotton pools of four million bales to be formed by the cooperatives in collaboration with bankers who would refuse loans to farmers unless they reduced cotton acreage by 25 percent and planted food and feeds. Southern governors were asked to proclaim "Cotton Reduction Week" in October, and a committee of bankers and agricultural leaders appeared in each state. The program had a more thorough follow-up even than that of 1921, and had the support of a special committee of three cabinet members with War Finance Corporation director Eugene Meyer as Chairman and $30,000,000 of credit available. Little of the money was used, but whatever the cause, six million fewer acres were harvested in 1927 and the average annual price rose above twenty cents again. . . .[83]

Whitfield's initiation of the Southern conference and the Cotton Conference show that he was not provincial in his position. He realized that Mississippi could not advance if her neighboring states did not also advance.

---

[82] Jackson *Daily Clarion-Ledger*, 18 March 1927.
[83] George Brown Tindall, *The Emergence of the New South 1913-1945*, in *A History of the South*, ed. Wendell Holmes Stephenson and E. Merton Coulter (Baton Rouge, 1961), p. 335; Mississippi *Laws* (1926), chap. 132.

In the area of recreation, the Governor never waned in his enthusiasm for golf. Unless there were pressing duties at home or trips out of town, his Saturday afternoons were devoted to this favorite hobby. An ardent baseball fan, he became one of the strong supporters of the Cotton States League. He attended the home games and encouraged all the state officials to support the home team. In 1925 he opened the baseball season by throwing in a baseball to Mayor Walter Scott.[84]

Whitfield's disposition toward people remained basically unchanged after he became Governor. He was always friendly and informal, never too busy to acknowledge anyone. Mrs. William L. Lowe encountered her former professor on the streets of Jackson one afternoon and said, "Oh, Mr. Whitfield, I am so happy to see you. I am so glad you were elected and Mississippi is blessed in having you for our governor." Whitfield replied, "Hester Luce, why don't any of my girls ever address me as Governor? You know they put me in the chair, come on, let's go to the mansion and have a cup of tea with the Governor's lady."

Another former student, Annie Denman, went to the city auditorium in Jackson to hear Whitfield speak. As he passed down the aisle he spotted her and, in the presence of a number of people, called out, "Howdy Annie!" This student remarked that he was always like that—"He could walk with kings but he never lost the common touch."

A humorous story serves to give additional insight into the Governor's disposition. Harry Smith, a student at Central High School in Jackson, enticed two of his friends to accompany him to the Governor's Mansion where they would request something to eat. Walking through Smith Park, they arrived at the back door of the Mansion to implement their mischievous plan. When a servant responded to their knock, they said, "We are hungry, could you give us something to eat?" It just happened that the Governor was walking past the door and heard the boys. He turned to them and said, "Hello boys, I was just getting ready to eat. Come in and have lunch with me." Though embarrassed

---

[84] Jackson *Daily News*, 8 May 1924; 13 April 1925.

by the development, the boys entered for lunch with the Governor.

Whitfield seemed to have been disillusioned about the Governor's office. He wanted people to respond with unselfish service to the state of Mississippi, and, he was disturbed when so many came to him requesting political favors with little interest in civic responsibility. He was disappointed that so many who called on him wanted personal advantage rather than opportunities for personal service to the state.

Governor Whitfield led the state in a progressive path. He gave his personal attention to the problems of the state, strengthened the forces of education, and sought to inform the people regarding matters related to the state. He promised honesty and integrity in government and abided by that promise. While seeking to be Governor of all the people, he was bold enough to call for better race relations. The Governor not only promoted the dairy industry; he promoted all industry in the state by encouraging the people to buy in Mississippi. He demonstrated his interest in other states by promoting the Cotton Conference and the Southern Governors' Conference. Attention is now turned toward the legislative program of the Whitfield administration.

4 · Legislative Program of the Whitfield Administration

Governor Whitfield's inaugural message sounded a clarion call to the legislature to deal with such measures as taxation, agriculture, industry, education, and highways. At this juncture in the Whitfield story attention is given to the legislative program and notable accomplishments of the Whitfield administration. When Whitfield came to the Governor's office the state was suffering because of unfair distribution of taxes; low prices of agricultural products; cutover forest lands without thought of replanting; declining population; attitude of big business toward the state; underdeveloped natural resources; and a deficit of $1,900,000 in the state treasury. Whitfield moved to make corrections in all of these areas.[1]

The Governor was no political craftsman, but he knew how to work with people. He leaned heavily upon Dennis Murphree, the Lieutenant Governor and a person with intimate knowledge of legislative procedure, for able assistance and advice. Murphree, as presiding officer of the Senate, chose the committee chairmen and appointed the committees in the Senate. "I gave the best men the jobs regardless," the Lieutenant Governor stated, "and the result was worthwhile for we had a harmonious session, and in the end were able to put over everything Governor Whitfield decided upon." The Governor was fortunate to have a legislature that was friendly and cooperative.[2]

---

[1] Mississippi *House Journal* (1924), pp. 210–33, 212; Columbus *Commercial Dispatch*, 7 January 1920; McLemore and McLemore, *Mississippi Through Four Centuries*, p. 294.

[2] "Memoirs of Dennis Murphree," chap. 33.

Governor Whitfield at desk in office

118 CATCH THE VISION

In addition to Murphree, Whitfield had the cooperation of four men who came to be called the "Big Four." They were Thomas Bailey, Walter Sillers, Joe George, and Lawrence Kennedy, all members of the state legislature. These men were friendly to the Governor and gave invaluable support in the passage of his legislative program. His means of communication with the legislature was through these influential men. Thomas Bailey, Speaker of the House, commented, "I am sure that our people have reason to rejoice that there is an administration in Jackson where the legislative and executive departments of the government are working hand in hand for the common good of all." [3] According to Murphree, Whitfield "never sought to use the big stick, or to drive folks. Truth is that he did not care to dominate or control people, and really cared less about official power than any man I have ever known in office." [4] In his approach to the legislature, Whitfield afforded a real contrast with his near contemporary, Huey Long of Louisiana. Regarding Long's approach to the legislature, T. Harry Williams said,

> On crucial bills he insisted on acting as his own floor leader. He would storm into either chamber and rush up and down the aisles barking out commands to his followers—move for passage or rejection; vote aye or nay. On a voice vote, he would sometimes himself answer for one of his adherents, bellowing the vote he wanted the man to cast.[5]

Whitfield was instrumental in moving Mississippi into the climate of business progressivism which characterized the South in the 1920s. Dewey Grantham wrote that "Southern progressivism had been transformed by the 1920s from the more militant anticorporation and political reform movement of the prewar period to what George B. Tindall has aptly called 'business progressivism.'" The following statement by Grantham will illustrate the climate of the South in the 1920s.

> In terms of efficiency and the public service concept of government there was a surprisingly vigorous reform movement in the

---
[3] Jackson *Daily News*, 30 January 1924.
[4] "Memoirs of Dennis Murphree," chap. 33.
[5] T. Harry Williams, *Huey Long* (New York, 1969), p. 298.

Legislative Program of the Whitfield Administration 119

South during the 1920s. A series of constructive governors, including Cameron Morrison of North Carolina, Bibb Graves of Alabama, and Austin Peay of Tennessee, achieved notable success in expanding public services and modernizing the machinery of state government. The development of highway programs and improved systems of education was spectacular in several southern states. Most of the southern states made phenomenal increases in expenditures for state services, introduced tax reforms and found new sources of revenue, created new administrative departments, developed their public health programs, and made significant progress in establishing welfare programs—this despite much talk about economy in government and laissez faire. Thus it is far from accurate to picture southern politics in the twenties, entirely in the somber colors of the Ku Klux Klan, prohibition, the Bible Belt fundamentalism, important as were these influences.[6]

As Whitfield's accomplishments are cited, it should be obvious that he was attempting to move Mississippi in the direction of the entire South, as described in the above quote from Grantham. Grantham's research should have led him to Henry Whitfield, who should have been included in his list of constructive governors in the South.

The first major task of the Governor was to put together an acceptable revenue and finance program. Dennis Murphree worked closely with Whitfield in this area and was a significant asset in the success of the financial program. Cecil Inman, an authority on taxes and taxation who had been employed by the United States Internal Revenue Department, was enlisted to draft the revenue program. Some of the measures were typed at least eight times before they were presented to the legislature.[7]

The Governor shared his theory of taxation with the citizens of Mississippi.

> The underlying idea of every tax is that the individual citizen derives protection from organized society; that is, from govern-

---

[6] Dewey W. Grantham, Jr., *The Democratic South* (Athens, 1963), p. 63; Tindall, *The Emergence of the New South 1913–1945*, p. 224.

[7] William D. McCain, "The Life and Labor of Dennis Murphree," *The Journal of Mississippi History* 12(1962):186; "Memoirs of Dennis Murphree," chap. 33.

ment. Not only are you protected in your life, your liberty, and your property by the government, but the government spends large sums in safeguarding your health, furnishing you conveniences of public utility, etc. It is fitting that in return for this service the citizen should support the government; in fact government is simply the instrument of the people and public officials the servants of the people. The people through their representatives tax themselves in order to provide revenue with which the public officials can perform the duties which the people, through their government, have enjoined upon them.[8]

In order to place the state on a solid financial foundation the Governor, ably assisted by Cecil Inman, set forth definite plans. Firmly convinced that the appropriations must remain within the revenues, Whitfield sent a scorching message to the legislature stating that no appropriation bills should be directed to him until enough money had been provided to cover the cost. His classic statement was, "Let us know how much cloth we have before we begin to cut the garments." The Governor urged the legislature to use the best business acumen and economy in determining all appropriations; furthermore, convinced that economy should begin at home, he urged the curtailment of local waste and extravagance.[9]

In 1924 the largest part of the state's revenue was derived from ad valorem taxes, with the bulk of the burden borne by the farmers and home owners. Whitfield called upon the legislature to rectify the situation by placing a proportional share of the tax burden upon the professions, businesses, and trades. He wanted the burden of taxation removed as far as possible from property and placed on privileges, luxuries, incomes, and profits.[10] The Governor's concern for the plight of the farmer and unfair taxation can be seen in the following statements.

> It might be well to call attention to the fact that this high tax on property has been an insufferable burden to the great majority of the poor people in the State of Mississippi. Most of these live

[8] H. L. Whitfield, *Know Mississippi*, p. 7.
[9] West Point *Leader*, 11 April, 1924; Mississippi *House Journal* (1924), pp. 215–17.
[10] Mississippi *House Journal* (1924), pp. 213–14.

on farms and their property is land. Farming has not been remunerative in the last few years, and great distress has been the portion of the great majority of the people who are providing the food and clothes for the human race; and yet under our obsolete form of taxation, these struggling people stagger under the awful load of taxation and have had to pay the larger part of the expenses of the State government and various interests fostered by the State.

It is the fundamental principle generally recognized and practiced among the Anglo-Saxon people, that the burden of taxation should be distributed among the people in proportion to their ability to pay taxes. . . . Notwithstanding that the farmers' profits are less than that of any other business, yet under the system which has heretofore reigned, he has had to stagger under the greater part of the burden of taxation.[11]

With the desire to spread the tax burden more equitably among the people of Mississippi, Whitfield recommended that the legislature levy taxes on soft drinks, tobacco, amusements, gasoline, lubricating oils, automobiles, income, lumber, and inheritance. He also added the following recommendations which were designed to promote economy and efficiency in state government: assess real and personal property in even years thus assuring that no property would be assessed in "political" years; provide for an annual or semiannual conference of the eighty-two tax assessors; determine a way to learn how much property in the state was exempt from taxation; show specific classification of all property which should be assessed; make the county assessor a full-time officer; and require all persons over twenty-one, who owned property, to submit an annual return stating the property owned and its value.[12]

Governor Whitfield wanted to abrogate every unnecessary office. He recommended the abolishment of the Revenue Agent and the transferral of his work to the State Tax Commission. He also recommended that the Attorney General receive a salary rather than the previous fifteen percent commission. The Governor called upon the legislature to create a general purchasing

[11] H. L. Whitfield, *State Finances* (Jackson, 1924), pp. 8–9.
[12] Mississippi *House Journal* (1924), pp. 215–16; Mississippi *Senate Journal* (1926), pp. 33–36.

board which would be the sole purchasing agent for the state institutions and to establish a uniform system of accounting.[13]

The cooperative climate of the legislature may be seen in the granting of practically all revenue requests of the Governor. In order to assure a better accounting of funds the legislature passed a law requiring greater accountability from the institutions, boards, and departments. The law provided that selected banks would receive, keep, and disburse, and correctly account for all funds of these agencies. An act was also passed requiring the heads of certain institutions, boards, and departments to file monthly reports with the State Auditor. The legislature passed an additional bill providing for a better system of withdrawing funds from the state treasury. To further strengthen the uniform system of accounting, an act was passed which provided for a more comprehensive system of bookkeeping by the State Highway Department.[14]

The legislature gave an overwhelming response to Whitfield's request for privilege taxation. A privilege tax was imposed on animal shows, circuses, menageries, side shows, and on each agency for the sale of waterwork plants, electric light plants, carbide plants, acetylene and other light plants of like nature, where the agency was established in the state or where such plants were kept on exhibition to induce sale. A privilege tax was also placed on: gasoline and oil dealers, hotels, bill posters, pay toilets, automobiles for hire, picture shows, automobile repair shops, automobile dealers, automobile accessories and tires, ferries, shoe repairing, any show or concert where fee was required and not devoted exclusively to religious, benevolent, or educational purposes, fruit peddlers, horse traders, firms conducting car washing, oiling stations, parking lots, upholstering shops, and painting and repair shops for vehicles of all kinds, liverymen and feedmen selling horses and mules, sawmillls, ped-

---

[13] Mississippi *Senate Journal* (1926), pp. 59–61; Mississippi *House Journal* (1924), pp. 216–17; and (1926), p. 238.
[14] Mississippi *Laws* (1924), chaps. 326, 327; and (1926), chaps. 169, 221. Unless otherwise noted all laws referred to in this chapter were passed in the Whitfield administration.

dlers of all kinds, foreign banking and trust companies, stock in foreign corporations, and dogs.[15]

Governor Whitfield was vitally interested in the roads in Mississippi, but he wanted those who used them to pay for them. Legislation was passed providing that the revenue derived from the sale of gasoline was to be divided equally between the state and the counties for the purpose of constructing and maintaining roads and highways.[16]

The success of these tax laws can be measured by the income from gasoline taxes alone. From 1 October 1923, to 30 September 1924, the total tax from gasoline was $851,997.67; from 1 October 1926, to 10 October 1927, the total tax from gasoline sales was $4,604,082.27. Of course there was an increase in the number of automobiles but the success of the tax is still obvious. The tax on gasoline was debated for two days in the Senate, but the problem was related to the use of the funds rather than the amount.[17]

Two other revenue bills of tremendous importance were those establishing the income tax and inheritance tax. These measures were suggested by Dennis Murphree, drafted by Cecil Inman, and sent to the legislature by Whitfield. In presenting the income tax measure Whitfield was following the steps of Louisiana Governor John M. Parker who had only recently led the Louisiana legislature to pass similar measures. The income tax bill levied a tax on individuals, partnerships, corporations, associations, trusts, and estates for the general fund of the state. The basic scale of the income tax began with the rate of one percent on the first thousand dollars of taxable income and gradually ascended to the rate of five percent on all taxable income in excess of twenty-five thousand dollars.[18] The Governor stressed the need of this legislation by stating:

---

[15] Ibid., chaps. 117–30.
[16] Ibid., chap. 115.
[17] *Biennial Report of the Auditor of Public Accounts of Mississippi* (1925), p. 135; (1927), p. 239; Jackson *Daily News*, 17 February 1924.
[18] "Memoirs of Dennis Murphree," chap. 33; Edwin Adams Davis, *Louisiana* (Baton Rouge), p. 335; Mississippi *Laws* (1926), chap. 132.

> Suppose you owned forty acres of land and worked this yourself; and an ad valorem tax is levied against this land even though poor crop conditions, insect pests, or the low price of farm products deprive you of all profit on your year's operation. Is it or not unfair that your brother who is a professional man or a skilled laborer, earning high wages and owning no property, should be required to pay a proportion of his income to the State by way of taxes. The land owner pays regardless of what he makes; under an income tax the citizen pays only in proportion to what he makes.[19]

The inheritance tax levied a transfer tax, for the benefit of the general fund of the state, on the net estates of decedents and on transfers and gifts made by a decedent. The basic scale of the tax began with the rate of one percent of the amount of the net estate not in excess of twenty-five thousand dollars, and gradually ascended to the rate of ten percent of the amount by which the net estate exceeded one million dollars. An inheritance tax was levied for the first time in Mississippi in 1918 but was superseded by the legislation of 1924. The revenue yield under the 1924 law more than doubled that under the 1918 law, which indicates the greater success of the 1924 legislation.[20]

The income tax and inheritance laws became the subject of much debate and criticism. Many believed that the Governor was leading Mississippi down a pioneer trail, to which he responded:

> Those who oppose income and inheritance taxes provided for . . . speak as though Mississippi were a pioneer State in levying taxes of this description. The truth is, Mississippi is tardy in the recognition of the fact that privileges and profits should bear a part of the burden of taxation. Forty-six out of forty-eight states have the inheritance tax law, and a large number of the States have the income tax law, and this number is increasing nearly as fast as legislatures meet. The modern world recognized the justice of such taxation with the result that there is

---

[19] Whitfield, *Know Mississippi*, pp. 13–14.
[20] Mississippi *Laws* (1924), chap. 134; M. C. Rhodes, *History of Taxation in Mississippi* (Nashville, 1930), pp. 125–27.

not a civilized country on the face of the globe which does not have income and inheritance tax laws.[21]

The income tax measure passed the legislature by a larger margin than many expected in light of the heated debate which surrounded the issue. In 1926 attempts to repeal the income and inheritance tax laws failed.[22]

Another important Whitfield request, related to revenue and taxation, to which the legislature acquiesced was the abolishment of the office of Revenue Agent and the creation of the office of State Tax Collector. Cecil Inman was appointed chaiman of the State Tax Commission.[23]

As a result of the Whitfield financial program, the state of Mississippi met its obligations from the revenues without issuing bonds for current expenses. This had not happened in many years. No doubt the Governor was pleased with this development for he had earlier raised the question, "Is it fair or not to your children to issue bonds for current expenses and leave them to redeem them?" [24]

A significant development of the Whitfield administration was the change in attitude and action toward industry and outside capital. The Governor had a vision of the industrial growth of Mississippi and was convinced that capital and industry could not be attracted by great natural resources alone. He wanted outside capital to feel secure in Mississippi with the assurance that its interest would be protected by the state. Whitfield called for justice and stability in dealing with outside investors. He did not want to surrender the sovereignty of the state in order to attract capital, but he did want to make the statutes just and their enforcement fair so that honest business would be attracted to Mississippi. He challenged the legislature to update all laws re-

---

[21] Whitfield, *State Finances*, 10.
[22] Jackson *Daily News*, 5 March 1924, 6 March 1924, 7 March 1924, 14 March 1924, 7 January 1926, 11 February 1926.
[23] Mississippi *Laws* (1926), chap. 286; Rowland, *The Official and Statistical Register*, p. 95.
[24] Rowland, *The Official and Statistical Register*, pp. 59-60; Whitfield, *Know Mississippi*, p. 9.

lated to industry. In dealing with capital, the "square deal" was a big notion with Whitfield. He was willing to give a square deal in return for a square deal.[25]

The governor had a vision of the day when large industrial centers of the state would provide a good market for the food crops raised by the farmers, thus resulting in prosperity for everyone. In his dream of diversified industry for Mississippi, Whitfield saw Mississippi cotton made into cloth in the state, and Mississippi's hardwoods, clay, cement, rocks, minerals, and other forms of natural wealth made into finished products within the borders of the state.[26]

The position of Mississippi's progressive leader was not clouded in doubt when he said, "We want our legitimate share of the new business investors who are looking to the South. . . ." In order to attract capital the Governor stated that the reputation of the state must reflect high ideals of political integrity and civic faith. He wanted all to know that capital would be welcomed and protected in Mississippi, but he also insisted that the relationship between the state and capital must be one of mutual cooperation rather than inexorable exploitation.[27]

When Whitfield came to the Governor's office, the image of Mississippi was anti-industry and pro-farmer. The administration of James K. Vardaman was "featured by laws attempting to curb the privileges which previous administrations had granted to railroads, lumber barons, and various corporations." He fought the trusts and combines that were attempting to move into the state to consume her natural resources.[28] This fear of outside exploitation had hindered the industrial advance of the state. Recalling the story of the Mississippi Power Company, A. J. Watson, Jr. states that for twenty years prior to the Whitfield administration there had been "hostile anti-industrial policy in both the Governor's office and the Legislature." Watson also said that

[25] Mississippi *Senate Journal* (1926), p. 104; Mississippi *House Journal* (1926), p. 123.
[26] Mississippi *House Journal* (1924), p. 1790, pp. 220–21.
[27] Mississippi *Senate Journal* (1926), p. 65; Mississippi *House Journal* (1924), pp. 220–21.
[28] Simkins, *A History of the South*, p. 542.

"the inauguration of Henry L. Whitfield in January, 1924 had inaugurated something more than a new Governor of Mississippi. It had brought a new and favorable climate for business and industry." [29]

In order to develop industrially the state needed cheap power. This prompted the Governor, who wanted to attract larger power plants to the state, to ask the legislature to repeal existing laws preventing the large companies from absorbing the smaller ones. Whitfield wanted to encourage the use of water by granting certain taxation immunities to plants operated by water power within the borders of Mississippi.[30]

In an attempt to attract capital to the state, Governor Whitfield made four other specific requests: rewrite the antitrust statute; entrust the State Tax Commission with authority to collect taxes on railroad, telephone, telegraph, and power companies operating within the state; give the Tax Commission authority to investigate delinquencies on the part of the taxpayers, and the auditing department sole authority to investigate official delinquencies among county and district officers and among officers and employees of all public institutions; invest only the Attorney General with the power to bring suits in the name of the state of Mississippi.[31]

The legislature manifested a spirit of cooperation and concern as the legislators sought to implement the Whitfield program concerning capital and industrial growth. An act was passed granting permission to any railroad to consolidate with any other railroad provided the same was organized and existing under the laws of the state of Mississippi and subject to the Interstate Commerce Act of Congress, and provided the consolidated company become a domestic corporation of the state of Mississippi.[32]

With the design of providing cheap power, an act was passed

---

[29] A. J. Watson, Jr., *Electric Power and People Power: The Story of the Mississippi Power Company* (New York, 1969), p. 9.
[30] Mississippi *House Journal* (1924), pp. 228-29, 1791.
[31] Mississippi *Senate Journal* (1926), p. 65.
[32] Jackson *Daily News*, 17 January, 1926; Mississippi *Laws* (1924), chap. 178.

giving the right of eminent domain to hydroelectric companies or corporations and associations organized for the purpose of developing the water power of rivers and streams for generators, distributing and selling electricity and electromechanical power for lighting, heating, and all purposes for which electricity could be used. The act empowered these companies to condemn and take necessary lands for the establishment of reservoirs, works, and rights-of-way.[33]

The legislature amended all laws necessary to pave the way for corporations to acquire the capital stock, franchise, plant, and equipment of other corporations. The law required that application be made to the Secretary of State, accompanied by information as to the purpose of the acquisition. This legislation was greatly desired by the Governor, but, in order to protect the state of Mississippi, provision was made for the resale of acquired stock should the acquisition be adverse to the public interest.[34]

Anxious to implement the Governor's legislative proposals related to industry, the legislature encouraged opening the doors of the state to factories that would make paper bags, paper boxes, and paper dishes, by exempting them from taxation for a period of five years. This was in direct response to the industrial dream of the Governor. Similar acts were passed in the interest of hardwood carbonizing and distillation plants that manufactured wood alcohol and other products from hardwood and hardwood waste, and new factories and new enterprises of public utility.[35]

The antiquated antitrust laws of Mississippi had been a hindrance to the industrial growth of the state prior to the Whitfield administration. In 1910 the legislature placed on the statute books a law that prohibited a corporation from owning over a million dollars in real estate or other assets. Because of this law industries of considerable size could not locate in Mississippi. It was generally believed that the Great Southern Lumber Company would have located in Mississippi, but it was forced to

[33] Mississippi *Laws* (1924), chap. 179.
[34] Ibid., chap. 182.
[35] Ibid. (1926), chaps. 163, 171, 172.

settle in Louisiana because of this legislation. Rumor had it that many of the oil and chemical industries that located at Baton Rouge, Louisiana, actually preferred Natchez, Mississippi, but this law prevented their coming. The Whitfield administration saw the repeal of this law which had so effectively aided in the industrialization of Louisiana. With the lifting of the million-dollar limit on assets, the state welcomed outside industry and capital. This repeal of the corporate holding law was recognized as an open invitation to foreign capital to invest in Mississippi and participate in the development of her resources.[36]

Governor Whitfield wanted outside capital to have opportunities within the state, but he also expected these business interests to respect and protect the privileges of Mississippi citizens. His position was accentuated by the following statement, made in connection with a suit against the Standard and Texas Oil Companies:

> I hope that I have made my position clear in the state of Mississippi in regard to the relation of the state to business. My acts and public utterances everywhere in the state clearly indicate my position. I think the state should deal fairly with all legitimate business so that no honest man could find any criticism with her laws or official acts; on the other hand I think that business should deal with Mississippi on the same high plane of fairness and justice.
>
> Where great corporations have been chartered to do business in the state they should be made to know that they must conduct their business according to the laws of the state, and if they do not obey the laws on the operations of their business they should be made to feel the strong arm of the state.
>
> In regard to the suit filed by the Attorney General I think that if the companies involved conspired together to so reduce the prices of gasoline below the market prices to make it impossible for a citizen of Mississippi to engage in business on a fair basis of competition in the sale of gasoline, then the time has come when Mississippi's legal authority should come to the

---

[36] Donald C. Mosley, "A History of Labor Unions in Mississippi" (Ph.D. dissertation, Mississippi State University, 1965), pp. 49–50; Jackson *Daily News*, 26 January 1924.

130 CATCH THE VISION

rescue of her citizens to see that at least they should have equal opportunity with outside companies to do business in Mississippi.[37]

Laws were passed imposing heavy penalties on a trust or combine that might have an adverse effect on the public welfare of the state. The legislation was especially intended to deal with any trust attempting to restrain trade, control commodity prices, control production and output, control commodity movement, and generally thwart the industrial progress in the state.[38]

Whitfield must be credited with bringing outside capital into Mississippi. Governor Hugh White later instituted his BAWI (Balance Agriculture With Industry) program, but it was Governor Whitfield who made it possible. Because of his attitude toward industrial growth, Whitfield may be called a disciple of Henry W. Grady, spokesman of the New South who encouraged the industrial advance of the South.[39]

The following statistics will show the effect of the Whitfield administration on foreign capital. The grand total of state and foreign capital to qualify in Mississippi for selected four-year periods was:

1916–19	State Capital	$ 41,114,800
	Foreign Capital	$229,480,000
	Total	$270,594,800
1920–23	State Capital	$ 49,141,210
	Foreign Capital	$ 62,907,400
	Total	$112,048,400
1923–27	State Capital	$ 67,682,930
	Foreign Capital	$815,907,890
	Total	$883,590,820[40]

It may be noted that the total foreign capital invested in Mississippi during the Whitfield administration increased in giant

---

[37] Jackson *Daily News*, 20 December 1925.
[38] Mississippi *Laws* (1926), chap. 182.
[39] Raymond B. Nixon, *Henry W. Grady, Spokesman of the New South* (New York, 1943), p. 332.
[40] *Biennial Report of the Secretary of State* (1927), p. 5.

proportion when compared to the two previous administrations. The economic advance of the Whitfield administration can also be observed by noting that the cash receipts in the office of the Secretary of State increased from $36,439 in 1923 to $61,697 in 1927.[41]

Another matter related to the industrial advance of the state was the "Stop, Look, and Listen" law, with which Governor Whitfield became closely identified. Concerned about the increase of collisions between automobiles and trains, the Governor wanted a law which would make it a misdemeanor when the driver of an automobile or truck crossed a railroad track without stopping. Consequently, the legislature passed a law requiring every motor vehicle to stop at least ten feet in front of the railroad track before crossing it. Signboards, reading MISSISSIPPI LAW—STOP, were to be painted white with red lettering and placed at every railroad crossing. These signs became symbolic of the state's new attitude toward outside industry and capital. The signs were saying that outside industry would be protected and given the right of way.[42]

The "Stop, Look, and Listen" law also served to remind outside investors of the responsibility which accompanied privilege. The law required every locomotive to have a bell of at least thirty pounds weight and a steam whistle that could be heard three hundred yards away. The bell was to be rung and the whistle blown at least three hundred yards before arriving at the place where the railroad crossed over any highway or municipal street.[43]

Throughout his career as an educator, Whitfield was always concerned about the physical health of the people and this did not change when he became Governor. He did not hesitate to call upon the legislature to consider seriously all physical needs. Not only did the Governor want the State Board of Health to have the money necessary to carry on its program for the pre-

[41] Ibid., p. 9.
[42] Mississippi *House Journal* (1924), p. 340; Mississippi *Laws* (1924), chap. 320.
[43] Mississippi *Laws* (1924), chap. 320.

vention of disease, but he also encouraged the legislators in any program designed to improve the health of Mississippians.[44]

When Governor Whitfield prepared the way for the relocation and rebuilding of the hospital for the mentally ill he reached the apex of all his achievements. He was convinced that the time had come when the location of this institution should be changed and a new facility built according to modern plans which had been worked out for the proper treatment of the insane. He suggested that the farm in Rankin County which was then owned and operated by the state for convicts become the site of the new hospital.[45]

The legislature agreed with the Governor regarding the needs of the mentally ill and passed an act to move the institution to Rankin County as he had suggested. The entire farm was reserved for the use of the state hospital and the way prepared for the disposal of the hospital property in Jackson. The name of the location was later changed from Howell to Whitfield in honor of the Governor. By giving attention to the mentally ill Whitfield was following in the steps of Napoleon Bonaparte Broward, Florida's progressive Governor, who had prodded his legislature to provide buildings and supplies for the state's mentally ill.[46]

Though young and inexperienced at the time, N. W. Overstreet, who later became a prominent architect in the state, approached the Governor with the possibility of his being commissioned to draw the plans for the new hospital. The young architect reminded Whitfield of a recent speech in which he stated that the day would come when it would not be necessary to go out of the state for professional services such as those offered by an architect. After the Governor concurred in having made the remarks, Overstreet replied, "Well, here I am." He got the job.

---

[44] Mississippi *House Journal* (1924), pp. 1543–46.
[45] Ibid. (1926), p. 200.
[46] Mississippi *Laws* (1926), chap. 115; Mississippi State Hospital, *Centennial Program* (n.p., 1955), p. 12; Samuel Proctor, *Napoleon Bonaparte Broward, Florida's Fighting Democrat* (Gainesville, 1950), pp. 231–32.

Governor Whitfield's last public address was made at the ground breaking for the first building of the new hospital. The event was reported by the Jackson *Daily News:*

> The climax of his long career of service was reached by the governor on that afternoon. Unable himself to turn the first spadefull of dirt for the largest building in the group for the new Mississippi State Hospital for the insane, the chief executive showed his great loyalty by making an appearance.
>
> In his opening remarks, Governor Whitfield declared his belief that from 30 to 40 percent of the insane patients of the state can be saved if given the proper treatment. With this in view, he stated that plans had been made to make the state institution second to none in the world. This view was in keeping with his unswerving belief that Mississippians are as good as any people on earth.[47]

Whitfield's secretary said he became a fanatic on the subject of this hospital. Dr. C. D. Mitchell, director of the hospital for many years, commented,

> Governor Whitfield did the outstanding deed of his life when he made it possible for this institution to be built for the insane unfortunates of this state. He will have built a monument to his memory that will last through the ages.[48]

Even though the hospital did not open its doors to receive patients until 1935, Whitfield did witness the beginning of construction.[49]

The legislature was eager to appropriate necessary funds for the expenses of the State Board of Health. Laws were passed which were designed to aid in the eradication of disease, and money was made available for the publication of literature on various health subjects. The Whitfield administration made changes in the State Board of Health relative to the manner of choosing the officers and their terms of service. The changes, which gave the Governor less power in the matter, were designed to keep the State Board of Health from becoming a

---

[47] Jackson *Daily News*, 18 March 1927.
[48] Ibid., 10 January 1927.
[49] Mississippi State Hospital, *Centennial Program*, p. 12.

134 CATCH THE VISION

political "football." Dr. Felix J. Underwood and Dr. R. N. Whitfield, who served as directors of the State Board of Health, commended the Whitfield administration for passing progressive health laws.[50]

Governor Whitfield was deeply concerned about the plight of the farmers in the state. He was convinced that something had to be done to make farming more profitable in order to bring about a farm life that would be more attractive to young men and women. In addition to his tax program, designed to afford relief to farmers, and his industrial development program, which would increase the market for farm products, Whitfield sought direct ways to assist the farmers. In response to his appeal for boll weevil control, the legislature made a sizable appropriation to the State Plant Board which was to be used to prevent the introduction and spread of the citrus boll weevil, citrus canker, sweet potato weevil, alfalfa weevil, European corn borer, Argentina ant, camphor scale, and other injurious insects, diseases, and pests.[51]

Since the farmers were afforded little protection in the purchase of seed, Governor Whitfield proposed and a measure was passed which provided for the production of cotton seed on the state farm at Parchman and the distribution of this seed to the cotton planters of the state. The superintendents of the state experiment stations at Stoneville and Holly Springs were to determine the variety which would be most profitable by means of test production at the experiment stations.[52]

One of the campaign promises of Whitfield was the establishment of grades and standards of farm products. His administration saw this promise become a reality when the Commissioner of Agriculture was authorized to establish grades and standards

---

[50] Mississippi *Laws* (1924), chaps. 15, 16, 304; Dallas Stewart, "Development of Public Health in Mississippi" (M. A. thesis, University of Mississippi, 1932), pp. 62-63; Felix J. Underwood and R. N. Whitfield, *Public Health and Medical Licensure in the State of Mississippi, 1798-1937* (Jackson, 1938), pp. 84-85.

[51] Mississippi *House Journal* (1924), pp. 218, 690-91; Mississippi *Laws* (1926), chap. 34.

[52] Mississippi *House Journal* (1924), pp. 690-91; Mississippi *Laws* (1926), chap. 273.

for farm products grown or produced in the state, using grades or standards established by the United States Department of Agriculture. This act enabled the Commissioner of Agriculture to investigate and certify to shippers and other financially interested parties the grade, quality, and condition of farm products shipped from the state.[53]

Two important pieces of legislation aided the farmer in obtaining needed financial assistance. The first, known as the Farmers' Credit Association, was designed to assist the farmers of the state through cooperative methods of obtaining credit for a longer period of time and at a lower rate of interest than was usually available to them. The second measure, known as the Mississippi Rural Credit Acts, provided a way for the farmer to have access to needed capital by means of the credit facilities of the Federal Intermediate Credit Bank in New Orleans.[54]

Governor Whitfield was anxious for the legislature to do something to rectify the problem of the depletion of forest lands in the state. Prior to his administration, thousands of acres of Mississippi forests had been cutover with no thought of reforestation. Nannie Rice reported to the *American Mercury* in 1926, "We are chagrined that others than ourselves garner our wealth; we feel consternation at the approach of its extinction. Almost before our eyes our long-leaf pine region is passing from the magnificent to the ugly, the trivial." A survey by United States foresters in 1908 revealed that more than fifty percent of the longleaf pine land of Mississippi had already been cutover. By 1920 many were beginning to realize that much of the land in South Mississippi would perhaps always be best suited to growing pine trees. The Governor wanted immediate action for the protection and conservation of forests; he further wanted a plan for the reforestation of lands.[55]

The Whitfield administration can lay claim to the creation of

---

[53] Mississippi *Laws* (1924), chap. 274.
[54] Ibid., chaps. 271, 272.
[55] Nannie H. Rice, "Mississippi," *The American Mercury* 7 (1926): 80; Nollie Hickman, *Mississippi Harvest: Lumbering in the Longleaf Pine Belt 1840–1915* (University, Mississippi, 1962), pp. 261, 265; Mississippi *House Journal* (1926), p. 381.

the State Forestry Commission, with duties of forestation, technical investigation and study, education and publication, management and protection. By the time of the biennial report of the Mississippi State Forestry Commission in 1927, the agency was already hard at work. During the fiscal year 1926–27, fifty-four meetings were held in rural communities of Mississippi, with more than 9,000 people in attendance. The extension forester chose to concentrate on a few counties in an effort to control forest fires. An example of the approach could be seen in the work done in Simpson County, where noticeable improvement was cited by the Mississippi State Forestry Commission in 1927.[56]

Another important measure related to the forest lands of the state was a law governing the growing of trees for manufacturing purposes on lands not useful for other profitable endeavors. This was an attempt to encourage individuals and corporations to utilize unimproved and unproductive lands for the purpose of growing trees which could be manufactured into lumber, wood pulp, paper, charcoal, fuel, or any other marketable finished product. The incentive behind this industry was the assurance that these lands would be assessed on the same basis as other unimproved and unproductive lands, and that the assessment of such lands would not be increased as a result of the reforestation and timber growth. The forests and trees which were grown under the provisions of this act were not to be subject to taxation for a period of ten years.[57]

Having taught in rural schools, served as State Superintendent of Education and President of Mississippi Industrial Institute and College, Governor Whitfield was naturally concerned about the problems of education in Mississippi. He considered all people to be the products of two factors—heredity and education, and so education was cited as a worthy interest of the state. The Governor's attitude toward education was included in his little book, *Know Mississippi:*

[56] *Biennial Report of the Mississippi State Forestry Commission* (1927), p. 19; Mississippi *Laws* (1926), chap. 161.
[57] Mississippi *Laws* (1924), chap. 329.

Under the conditions of modern civilization, the maintenance of a system of education for all the people is absolutely indispensable. As society becomes more complex, the need not only of more schools, but the importance of having each kind of school worked out to meet the needs for which it was established, becomes more important.[58]

An educational highlight of the Whitfield administration came when the legislature passed an act making an appropriation for the support, maintenance, and furnishings for the Delta State Teachers' College. Whitfield had longed to see a college established in the Delta and had enthusiastically promoted the idea. He was overjoyed when the opportunity came to sign the bill which created the college. During the process of establishment and organization, he was very active—attending various meetings and offering support in every way. Mrs. William Marion Kethley, whose husband became President of Delta State College in 1926, said the college was "Mr. Whitfield's brain child." It must be recognized that many believe the state of Mississippi would have been helped in a greater way if money had been used to improve the facilities of the existing colleges rather than to establish a new college.[59]

Governor Whitfield had maintained a genuine interest for many years in the Mississippi Normal College at Hattiesburg. During his administration the name of the college was changed to the State Teachers' College. He one day remarked, "This great undeveloped section of our state! We need more people, more money, and there ought to be a great college here of three or four thousand students with improved and expanded facilities." It appears that his vision obviously anticipated the impressive campus and large student body of the University of Southern Mississippi today. While Whitfield was promoting the growth of the State Teachers' College and the establishment of Delta State

---

[58] Whitfield, *Know Mississippi*, pp. 21–22.
[59] Winston, *A Sampler*, p. 104; William Marion Kethley, "A Brief History of Delta State College," *The Journal of Mississippi History* 19 (1957): 174–75. The name of Delta State College was changed to Delta State University in 1974.

College, Austin Peay, Governor of Tennessee, was leading his state in the creation of Austin Peay Normal (later changed to Austin Peay State University) at Clarksville.[60]

The educational and cultural life of the state was considerably enhanced as the result of an act which created the State Library Commission. According to the provisions of this act, the commission would be available to advise all schools, free and other public libraries, and all communities proposing to build libraries, as to the best means of establishing and maintaining such libraries. The commission was also granted the authority to operate traveling libraries which could circulate among communities, schools, colleges, library associations, study clubs, and charitable and penal institutions. The commission was authorized to obtain reports from all libraries in the state showing their condition, growth, and development.[61]

The High School Textbook Commission was created during the Whitfield administration. The commission was given the duties of arranging a program of studies for each type of high school and adopting the textbooks to fit the respective program of studies. The selected books were to be sold to Mississippi patrons at prices comparable to other areas of the United States. Evidently the legislature was determined that the students use the books because a law was passed authorizing the trustees of municipal separate school districts containing a municipality of not less than ten thousand population to employ a truant officer, or officers, to enforce the state compulsory school.[62]

Governor Whitfield was concerned about constructing and maintaining good roads. Governor Austin Peay, Whitfield's contemporary and counterpart in Tennessee, was leading his state in such remarkable progress in this area that he was called "the Roadbuilding Governor."[63] Critical of the fact that Missis-

---

[60] Mississippi *Laws* (1924), chap. 295; Robert E. Corlew, Stanley J. Folmsbee, and Enoch L. Mitchell, *Tennessee, A Short History* (Knoxville, 1969), p. 491.
[61] Mississippi *Laws* (1926), chap. 180.
[62] Ibid., chaps. 316, 317.
[63] Corlew, et al., *Tennessee*, p. 491.

Legislative Program of the Whitfield Administration 139

sippi had wasted large sums of money because of the failure to maintain the roads, Whitfield did not want to consider building additional roads until adequate maintenance was assured. Speaking of the importance of good highways, the Governor said,

> Discuss the building of famous roads in history and tell of the influence which trade routes and military roads have had in the development of nations and the spread of civilization. For example, read up on the roads of Babylon, Egypt, Greece, Rome, France, and England. Tell of the road building activities of Caesar, Hannibal, Napoleon, and the Germans and Allies of the Great War. Acquaint yourself with the romantic stories of the Oregon Trail, the Santa Fe Trail, and the Natchez Trace. Is it true or not that soldiers of the American Army traveled over roads built in France two thousand years ago by Caesar and his legions? As a younger nation do we not derive valuable lessons on the importance of permanent road construction from the experience of the older nations.[64]

Judge N. S. Sweat, prominent Corinth attorney who served in the legislature during the Whitfield administration, stated that the Governor wanted good roads and the legislature wanted to cooperate with him in this desire. The state's chief executive envisioned good roads that would bring the "farmer closer to his market, his family closer to the conveniences of town, his children within reach of the consolidated school." [65]

A major accomplishment of the legislature during the Whitfield administration was an act to establish, create, and define a system of state highways. This highway system was designed to connect the county seats of the state. Prior to this time there was no organized highway system in the state. The Governor was very anxious to stop the haphazard approach to road construction. This new highway system was placed under the supervision of the Mississippi State Highway Department. The desire of Whitfield for a better system of state highways

[64] Whitfield, *Know Mississippi*, p. 91.
[65] Ibid., p. 92.

reflects the attitude of North Carolina's Governor Cameron Morrison, who was known as the "Good Roads Governor."[66]

To further assist in the creation of a better highway system in the state, a law was passed which prescribed the width of all bridges and culverts on the public roads. Culverts were to be the full width of the crown of the roadway and never less than sixteen feet wide. When Whitfield became Governor of Mississippi, there was no uniform system of marking the public roads in the state; the legislature passed an act to provide this service.[67]

The legislative and court records reveal that in 1924 the state's penal system had been a constant source of legal friction and political agitation. Governor Whitfield had a compassionate heart for the criminal and sought constructive assistance for him in addition to punishment for the crime of which he was guilty. The Governor wanted the inmates of the penitentiary to live under comfortable and hygienic conditions, free from communicable diseases. He desired that the prisoners have opportunities that would enhance their physical and moral development. In an attempt to move the prison as far away from politics as possible, the Governor stated that any employee of the prison who made a contribution to the political campaign of any person should be fired. He longed to see the penitentiary farm become a successful experiment station and a commendable example of progressive farming.[68]

Governor Whitfield stated that in dealing with the offenders against society, two distinct ends should be kept always in view. The first was to decrease in every conceivable way the number of offenders against society's laws in the future. The second goal was to help the unfortunate offender in every possible way to get a new vision of the possibilities and responsibilities of life and to prepare him more adequately to meet these responsibilities and realize these possibilities following his release from prison. Suc-

---

[66] Mississippi *Laws* (1926), chap. 218; Hugh Talmadge Lefler and Albert Ray Newsome, *North Carolina* (Chapel Hill, 1954), p. 531.
[67] Mississippi *Laws* (1926), chaps. 223, 224.
[68] Mississippi *House Journal* (1924), pp. 229-30.

Whitfield being welcomed to MGM studios (above) while attending United States Good Road Association convention in Santa Monica, California—(below) Whitfield, shown second from left with other Governors attending convention

cinctly stated, he wanted to turn the offender into an asset to the state rather than a liability.[69]

The Governor had some definite suggestions designed to assist in the rehabilitation of the criminal. He wanted all first offenders to be separated from the repeaters. The progressive concept of Henry Whitfield can readily be seen in his desire to introduce the convicts to some trade other than farm work. He called upon the penitentiary leadership to consider such trades as carpentry, brick masonry, cabinet work, shoe repairing, weaving, and other practical arts and crafts. Prisoners having special aptitudes for these trades could have an opportunity to receive such training while rendering service to the state. In this manner the offender could acquire an increased earning power which would be a strong incentive for a law-abiding life following his release.[70]

Whitfield wanted the inmates to be surrounded by the very best of conditions during the period of their incarceration. At this point there was no vagueness in his desires. He plainly called for the best sanitary conditions in all of the buildings and insisted that the laws of personal hygiene be carefully observed. He wanted the food to be nourishing and plentiful; the treatment to be firm, kind, and considerate. Desiring to make the convict a better man with higher ideals, the Whitfield program called for moral, intellectual, and religious instruction for all prisoners. The Governor also wanted those suffering from tuberculosis or other communicable diseases to remain in isolation.[71]

With emphasis upon helping the prisoner, Whitfield was performing in accordance with a widespread reform movement which was seeking such improvements. Hoke Smith, Governor of Georgia and later United States Senator, was one of the leaders who encouraged improvement in the state prisons. Westmoreland Davis, who was elected Governor of Virginia in 1917, also called for several prison reforms including better medical attention, better facilities and a stronger elementary

---

[69] Ibid. (1926), p. 360.
[70] Ibid., pp. 360–61.
[71] Ibid., pp. 361–62.

education program. The actions initiated by Whitfield, Smith, and Davis were in response to the humanitarian sentiment which the South was beginning to demand.[72]

The Whitfield administration accomplished two things which noticeably affected penitentiary life. First, Whitfield made good his promise that the superintendent in charge of the penitentiary would be one of the most experienced and progressive farmers in the state. T. L. Fox, able and experienced head of the Delta Pine and Land Company's enormous cotton plantations, took a leave of absence in an attempt to make Parchman a model penitentiary and a valuable income-producing asset for the state. Second, through the insistence and inspiration of Whitfield, an act was passed which appropriated $12,500 for the purpose of building and equipping a hospital for the Parchman state farm.[73]

The prison report for 1927 indicated definite improvements at Parchman. Four modern brick units had been constructed and equipped with modern sanitary bathrooms. There was a great improvement in the management and treatment of the prisoners which was attributed to the new superintendent and sergeants. The health of the convicts was very good as a result of better sanitary conditions and the professional treatment by Dr. W. P. McDavid and other able physicians. The prison superintendent was pleased with the progress of the penitentiary reforms according to his biennial report in 1927.[74]

Because Governor Whitfield wanted Mississippi to be a law-abiding state, he was a strong advocate of law enforcement. Whitfield was especially anxious to deal with those who were contemptuous of the prohibition laws. The legislature passed several laws relative to alcoholic beverages. One act was designed to simplify the procedure of obtaining search warrants where there was suspicion of violation of the prohibition laws. The law provided that any justice of the peace, judge of the

---

[72] Dewey W. Grantham, Jr., *Hoke Smith and the Politics of the New South* (Baton Rouge, 1958), p. 174; Jack Temple Kirby, *Westmoreland Davis, Virginia Planter-Politician 1859-1942* (Charlottesville, 1968), p. 102.
[73] Mississippi *Laws* (1924), chap. 43.
[74] *Biennial Report of the Board of Trustees Superintendent and Others of the Mississippi State Penitentiary* (1925), p. 3; and (1927), pp. 3-4.

circuit court, or chancellor of the district in which these violations occurred could issue such a warrant upon the affidavit of any credible person that he had reason to suspect a violation of the law.[75]

The legislature passed an act making it unlawful for any person or corporation to own or operate any distillery known as a "still." Another act was passed increasing the bond for violation of any of the criminal statutes prohibiting the sale and possession of intoxicating liquors. In addition to the laws relative to intoxicating beverages, the Whitfield administration gave tangible expression of concern about the use and abuse of drugs. A law was passed which was intended to regulate the sale of cocaine, opium, morphine, and their derivatives and compounds.[76]

The Whitfield administration took a hard-line stand against gambling. Legislation was passed making it unlawful for any person or firm to operate a cane rack, knife rack, punch board, slot machine, or similar devices.[77]

An additional asset for strict law enforcement was the act which authorized the boards of supervisors in counties having an assessed valuation of twenty-five million dollars to employ, at their discretion, patrolmen to enforce the road and motor vehicle laws. Another measure designed to promote better law enforcement was the act authorizing photographs and fingerprints of persons charged with felony.[78]

The creation of county courts was another commendable feature of the Whitfield administration. This law provided that in counties with a population of at least 35,000 or with an assessed valuation of real and personal property exceeding seventeen million dollars, and in either case having a municipality of 5,000, an inferior court known as the county court was to be

---

[75] Mississippi *House Journal* (1924), pp. 231-32; Mississippi *Laws* (1924), chap. 244.
[76] Mississippi *Laws* (1924), chaps. 245, 246, 248.
[77] Ibid., chap. 339.
[78] Ibid. (1926), chaps. 165, 202.

Legislative Program of the Whitfield Administration 145

established. This court was to have jurisdiction concurrent with the courts of justices of peace in all matters, civil and criminal. The county court was also to have jurisdiction concurrent with the circuit and chancery courts in all matters of law and equity where the value involved did not exceed one thousand dollars. The county court system was established in thirteen counties in Mississippi. The result was a speeding up of the trial of a number of cases. There were those who expected the county court to bring an end to the justice of the peace system, but this has not happened.[79]

Even though the Governor wanted greater economy in government, he was unwilling to reduce the assistance offered through the eleemosynary institutions, such as schools for the blind and deaf. He also wanted the officials and employees of the eleemosynary institutions to be selected because of special fitness for the place and not because of political expediency. Whitfield frowned upon using these institutions as opportunities for political reward; he viewed the granting of positions to relatives and undeserving friends as a crime against society. The legislature responded to this concern by passing an act which made nepotism unlawful in state, county, and municipal appointive or elective offices.[80]

Governor Whitfield was always eager for all the veterans to receive the gratitude of the state in abundant measure. In addition to his active support of the American Legion, he requested the legislature to pass a law for the immediate creation of a State Service Commissioner, who would have the responsibility of helping all residents of the state who had served in the military forces of the United States. The service officer was to assist the veterans, their relatives and dependents, in receiving all due benefits from the United States government. He was also to assist the United States government by exposing all unjust claims for benefits. R. D. Morrow, who was appointed by Whitfield as

---

[79] Ibid., chap. 131; Jackson *Daily News*, 21 March 1926.
[80] Mississippi *House Journal* (1924), p. 227; Mississippi *Laws* (1926), chap. 170.

146   CATCH THE VISION

Governor Henry L. Whitfield, at dedication of Mississippi Veterans Home

the first service commissioner, stated that prior to this time the veterans had no genuine representation and some people would take advantage of them.[81]

Whitfield loved the coastal area of Mississippi and felt that this section could never realize its full potential without the construction of a sea wall. Convinced that the state had "no greater asset than this wonderful section," he brought the matter of the sea wall before the people. Even though many other people were involved, the influence of Henry Whitfield was certainly felt when the voters of Harrison County passed a bond issue of $1,400,000 for the purpose of building the fourteen-mile wall.[82]

In October 1926 Governor Whitfield began to experience pain in his hip and knee. Following his physician's advice, he visited Hot Springs, Arkansas, in search of relief from suffering. The trip was futile. Within two weeks a growth was discovered on

[81] Mississippi *Laws* (1924), chap. 321.
[82] Mississippi *House Journal* (1924), p. 1160.

Legislative Program of the Whitfield Administration 147

the femur, just above the knee. He was sent to Campbell's Clinic in Memphis, where the difficulty was diagnosed as bone cancer. Friends had become concerned over his obvious decline in health, especially the loss of over twenty-five pounds in weight. The malignant bone disease possibly resulted from a fall which he received while playing tennis at II&C.[83]

On 1 December, the Governor's left leg was amputated several inches above the knee. He was very stoic about the whole affair. During the long days of recovery, he enjoyed working crossword puzzles as he lay in bed. He welcomed visitors but did not want attention focused on himself. Miss Emma Hooper, a former student, spoke of her visit with him: "Though I tried to lead him to talk about himself and his work, he kept me answering questions about my work and the progress of education in North Carolina. He was still the kindly man and the great educator." [84]

The Governor had sufficiently recovered by 6 January to leave the hospital and return to Jackson. State officials and other friends greeted him when he arrived on the Illinois Central passenger train. The city was gaily decorated for the occasion; the Jackson Boy's Band escorted him to the Mansion which had been prepared for his arrival. Whitfield had been absent since 12 October when he left for the Cotton Conference.[85]

Governor Whitfield was able to walk with the aid of crutches; thus limited attention could be given each day to his official responsibilities. Several visitors were received during this time, one of whom was a member of the State Board of Law Examiners. The Governor wanted to discuss the possibility of his taking the examination which would pave the way for a future law practice. Obviously he thought the disease had been arrested and plans should be made for his future employment. He was encouraged to think he might have the opportunity of associating with one of the Jackson law firms.

[83] Meridian *Star*, 14 March 1927; Jackson *Daily News*, 28 November 1926; 30 November 1926.
[84] Jackson *Daily News*, 1 December 1926.
[85] Jackson *Daily News*, 6 January 1927.

148 CATCH THE VISION

Whitfield tried very hard to remain active, but it soon became evident that his health was failing. One afternoon as he was leaving the office, he turned and said, "Good-by you all." This was the first time he had ever said "Good-by" to the office staff. They knew what he meant—he was never to return to the office again. For the first time in his official life, visitors were told they could not see the Governor. No secretary or "buffer" had ever barred entrance to the Mansion or executive office during his administration. The farmer, with his, "howdy Guv-nor," was welcomed as readily as the statesman.[86]

As the situation became worse, the Governor experienced only short periods of consciousness. During one of these periods he shared with the family his desire for a simple funeral without any lavish display. He requested that his military staff serve as pallbearers, and that only the state flag of Mississippi be placed on the casket. Mrs. Whitfield was constantly at his bedside. The Negro servants, upon hearing that death was imminent, went to the rear yard and dropped on their knees in fervent prayer. He died at 4:41 a.m., 18 March 1927.[87]

According to the request of the Governor, funeral rites, held in the capitol building at 10 o'clock, were brief and simple. Three hymns were sung—"Lead, Kindly Light," "Beautiful Isle of Somewhere," and "Over There." The memorial sermon was delivered by Dr. W. A. Hewitt, Whitfield's pastor and friend. Following are some of his remarks.

> We have never seen a day like this. For 94 years no governor of this State has fallen in office, so on this occasion we are passing through a new experience. Regardless of age or condition of factional alliance, we meet today upon a common ground to pay loving tribute to a good man and a great governor.
>
> He was a man who cared more for practice than for profession. He had little faith in education that was not practical. He had little confidence in a profession of religion that was not demonstrated in practice.
>
> He put service above self. Service was the passion of his whole life. No one ever heard him contend for his rights. He

[86] Memphis *Commercial Appeal,* 18 March 1927.
[87] Jackson *Daily News,* 17 March 1927; 18 March 1927.

Legislative Program of the Whitfield Administration 149

was willing to contend for the rights of others, but not his own. He loved to serve and he served his beloved State with every fibre of his being, with every ounce of his strength and with every drop of his blood that flowed through his heart.

He cared more for sincerity than for social prestige or any other advantage. He never said one thing and meant another, but always meant what he said. Honesty and sincerity were dominant characteristics of his life.

He loved humanity and despised haughtiness. With all his success he was unspoiled. . . . He chose sacrifice rather than personal success. He was willing to give up his savings of a life time and most of his life insurance rather than call on his friends for campaign contributions. He was willing to become poor that we through his poverty might be rich. He gave his all to Mississippi, that he loved better than his own life. He gave himself in sacrificial and strenuous service that weakened his body and made it an easy prey for disease. So he gave his life as a loving sacrifice for us.[88]

Following the service the body was removed to Columbus for burial. Dr. Hewitt and the Reverend J. D. Franks read the Scripture and prayed; A. H. Doty sang, "Sometime We'll Understand."

Hundreds of eulogistic statements were forthcoming. Will Rogers said

He was a plain, lovable character and he handed me out much homely philosophy. I will miss him next year when I go back, and his State will him. He was just a plain Governor of the great State of Mississippi. You missed a lot by not knowing Governor Whitfield. We don't raise any more like him, for conditions have changed.[89]

And others said

Glorious things can be said of his devotion to duty, holy ambition, high idealism, broad scholarship, strength of mind, unselfishness of purpose, wealth of friends, and ability in statesmanship. But best of all we delight to know of his humble discipleship as a follower of the Son of God, his purity of heart,

[88] Winona *Times*, 25 March 1927.
[89] Will Rogers, New York *Times*, 21 March 1927, 21:7.

150 CATCH THE VISION

PICTURE COURTESY OF MRS. CECIL INMAN

The body of Governor Whitfield being removed from state capital for burial in Columbus

his devotion to his church, his consistence and spirituality as a Christian.[90]
Henry L. Whitfield, probably the most popular governor in the history of Mississippi, is dead.[91]
If there has been one word of scandal against this man, remarkable as it may seem to say of a man who has held the merciless spotlight of high station—I have never heard it. More, he has been faithful to his trust.[92]
No Mississippian will ever feel the blush of shame because of the administration of H. L. Whitfield.[93]

Clayton Rand, prominent Gulf Coast newspaperman, penned the following poem in honor of Whitfield.

His was a courageous soul
Crusading for the things that count.
His heart went out to make the art
of mother-craft one more complete.
He taught the curriculum
of character and vision.

[90] The Reverend Roland Q. Leavell, *The Church Chimes*, First Baptist Church Picayune, Mississippi, 20 March 1927, 1.
[91] Memphis *Press Scimitar*, 18 March 1927.
[92] Jackson *Daily Clarion-Ledger*, 19 March 1927.
[93] Grenada *Sentinel*, 18 March 1927.

Instructor of mind and heart
His teachings also touched the souls
Of Mississippi's girls and boys,
and homes are happier that
He lived and loved and labored
To inspire the sons of men.
He brought the cleansing power
of high ideals to state-craft,
and Mississippians feel a sense
of pride in purer suffrage.
By raising service above self
He now rests with time's immortals;
No tribute fitting to describe
His works other than his noble life;
No homage more deserving than
The confidence he quickened in
A New State Consciousness.

When Governor Whitfield wrote his book, *Know Mississippi*, he included "The Man Who Counts," which had been written by Theodore Roosevelt. The description of the man who counts is a description of Henry Whitfield.

> It is not the critic who counts, nor the man who points out how the strong man stumbles, or where the doer of deeds could have done better. The credit belongs to the man who is actually in the arena; whose face is marred by dust and sweat; who strives valiantly; who errs and may fail again and again, because there is no effort without error and shortcoming, but who does actually strive to do the deeds; who does know the great enthusiasm, the great devotion; who spends himself in a worthy cause; who, at the best, knows in the end the triumph of high achievement, and who at the worst, if he fails, at least fails while daring greatly, so that his place shall never be with those cold and timid souls who know neither victory nor defeat.[94]

Henry Whitfield was "The Man Who Counts." Discontent to occupy the seat of a spectator, his vision carried him into the arena where he experienced the triumph of high achievement. In addition to the personal influence which he exerted over the lives of many people, his laurels of victory are displayed for all to see.

[94] Whitfield, *Know Mississippi*, 3.

152 CATCH THE VISION

As State Superintendent of Education his missionary work for schools began a movement that afterwards developed into a stronger system of public education. He led the state to move forward in vocational training, physical education, and teacher training. He spurred the establishment of agricultural high schools and the textile school at Mississippi Agricultural and Mechanical College.

As President of Mississippi Industrial Institute and College, campus, curriculum, and faculty improvements resulted in an increase in the graduating class from 23 to 129. Also in the arena of education Delta State College and the University of Southern Mississippi are marked by his influence. He assisted Piney Woods School to overcome its difficult days.

In the governing of Mississippi Whitfield had many achievements. As Governor he created an image of integrity for Mississippi and placed the state on a solid financial foundation. He opened the door for the industrial advance of Mississippi. At least a portion of the honor that has been heaped upon Hugh White for the BAWI program should be shared with Henry Whitfield. Through the establishment of the State Forestry Commission, he set the state on the course of conservation and reforestation which has resulted in the giant timber industry.

The Mississippi State Hospital stands today as a worthy memorial to the humanitarian disposition of Henry Whitfield. As a deeply religious person he was a valuable ally of every Christian cause; he especially left his mark on the work of Mississippi Baptists.

When Mississippians reflect upon their past history, they can look with pride and appreciation to the life and accomplishments of Henry L. Whitfield—who *caught the vision!*

Appendix A · Genealogy of Henry Lewis Whitfield

From first generation recorded in America:

Matthew Whitfield, only records 1682, married Priscilla Lawrence, Nansemond County, Virginia; among their issue

William Whitfield I, born about 1690, married Elizabeth Goodman, about 1713; among their issue

William Whitfield II, born May 29, 1715, married Rachel Bryan, November 6, 1741; among their issue

Reverend Lewis Whitfield, born June 23, 1766, married Charlotte Bryan; among their issue

"Sir" William Whitfield, date of birth unknown, married Elizabeth Wimberly; their only issue

George William Whitfield, born December 1, 1808, married Catherine Diggs Hart; among their issue

Robert Allen Whitfield, born January 11, 1839, married July 3, 1860, Mollie Fitzhugh; among their issue

Henry Lewis Whitfield, born June 21, 1868, Rankin County, Mississippi, married Mary White.

* Genealogical information courtesy Mrs. Harry Artz Alexander, Grenada, Miss.

Bibliography

I. ORIGINAL SOURCES

A. BOOKS AND PAMPHLETS

Announcing the Henry Lewis Whitfield Scholarship Fund. Mississippi State College for Women, 1 July 1963.
Whitfield, H. L., "A Greater Mississippi," *Four Masterpieces On Education, Unionism and Labor Problems.* Edited by W. W. Welch, pp. 25–36. Jackson, n. d.
⸺. *Going Off To College.* n. p., 1914.
⸺. *Know Mississippi.* Jackson, 1925.
⸺. *State Finances.* Jackson, 1924.

B. PERIODICALS

Whitfield, H. L., "A Message From Governor Whitfield." *The Mississippi Educational Advance* 15(1924):8, 46.
⸺. "An Address by State Superintendent H. L. Whitfield." *Proceedings of the Mississippi Teachers Association* (May 1905), pp. 134–38.
⸺. "Industrial Education." *The Mississippi School Journal* 14(1910):7–10.
⸺. "Program for 'Mississippi Day.'" *The Mississippi School Journal* 6(1902):629–30.
⸺. "Standards in Education." *The Mississippi School Journal* 14(1909):23–29.
⸺. "The Field of Activity for the Normal College." *The Mississippi Educational Advance* 1(1911):5–8.
⸺. "The Teachers' Reading Course." *The Mississippi School Journal* 14(1909):1–5.
⸺. "The Teachers' Reading Course." *The Mississippi School Journal* 14(1909):7–10.

C. MANUSCRIPTS AND COLLECTIONS

Columbus, Miss. Mississippi State College for Women. "History of Mississippi State College for Women" [by Sarah D. Neilson].
―――――. Mississippi State College for Women. John Clayton Fant Memorial Library. H. L. Whitfield Correspondence.
―――――. Mississippi State College for Women. John Clayton Fant Memorial Library. A. B. Schauber Correspondence.
―――――. Mississippi State College for Women. Alumnae Office. "History of Mississippi State College for Women."
―――――. Mississippi State College for Women. Alumnae Office. Emma Ody Pohl Papers.
―――――. Mississippi State College for Women. Alumnae Office. H. L. Whitfield Scholarship Folder.
Jackson, Miss. Dennis Murphree Memoirs. In possession of Mary Frances Murphree Ford.
―――――. Field Co-Operative Association. "Field Co-Operative Association Inc., 1919–1946."
―――――. Mississippi Department of Archives and History. Harry Bryan Scrapbook. 2 vols. 1923.
―――――. Mississippi Department of Archives and History. A. J. McLaurin Collection. Series E.
―――――. Mississippi Department of Archives and History. J. T. Ruble's unpublished account of the Wisconsin Trip.
―――――. Mississippi Department of Archives and History. H. L. Whitfield Correspondence, subject folder.
Pickens, Miss. Whitworth Scrapbook. In possession of Mary Massey Whitworth.
Plain, Miss. Edgar Misterfeldt Diary. In his possession.
State College, Miss. Mississippi State University. Mitchell Memorial Library. J. C. Hardy Papers, 1900–1912.
―――――. Mississippi State University. Mitchell Memorial Library. Nannie Herndon Rice Collection.
Tupelo, Miss. Robert Allen Whitfield Papers. "Sketch of Henry Whitfield's Life," and "Memoirs of Robert Allen Whitfield," 2 vols. In possession of Henry M. Whitfield.

D. PERSONAL COMMUNICATION

Interviews

Amis, Attorney A. B., Newton, Miss., 20 April 1971.
Alexander, Mrs. Harry Artz, Grenada, Miss., 15 December 1970.

Atkinson, Floyd, Newton, Miss., 23 April 1971.
Atwell, Miss Etta, Columbus, Miss., 15 March 1971.
Bilbo, Mrs. Theodore G., Jackson, Miss., 13 November 1970.
Bullock, Mrs. Mary, Florence, Miss., 9 April 1971.
Butler, Mrs. Gertrude, Sunflower, Miss., 8 January 1971.
Carr, Mrs. R. B., Pontotoc, Miss., 12 December 1970.
Chaney, Mark, Edwards, Miss., 19 March 1971.
Corley, Si, Jackson, Miss., 19 March 1971.
Crouse, W. E., Columbus, Miss., 15 March 1971.
Daniels, W. P., New Albany, Miss., 2 August 1971.
Doty, A. H., Jackson, Miss., 19 March 1971.
Eastland, Senator James O., Doddsville, Miss., 8 January 1972.
Eggers, Jim, Columbus, Miss., 15 March 1971.
Ellard, Mrs. J. A., Pittsboro, Miss., 6 January 1971.
Evans, Carless J., Meridian, Miss., 22 April 1971.
Evans, Dr. Clytee R., Columbus, Miss., 15 March 1971.
Ewing, Dr. J. M., Clinton, Miss., 4 September 1971.
Glass, Attorney David H., Kosciusko, Miss., 10 December 1970.
Graham, Merle, Columbus, Miss., 15 March 1971.
Gregory, Mrs. L. H., Aberdeen, Miss., 6 November 1970.
Guyton, Mrs. Grady, Oxford, Miss., 16 January 1971.
Halbert, Mrs. Mary Foote, Birmingham, Ala., 5 March 1971.
Hammond, Miss Hattie, Grenada, Miss., 15 December 1970.
Henley, Attorney W. S., Hazlehurst, Miss., 19 March 1971.
Hewitt, Purser, Jackson, Miss., 10 November 1969.
Hudson, Archie, Collins, Miss., 19 March 1971.
Hudson, Larue, Collins, Miss., 19 March 1971.
Inman, Mrs. Cecil, Jackson, Miss., 18 March, 1971.
Ivy, Dr. H. M., Meridian, Miss., 5 August 1971.
Jones, Lawrence C., Piney Woods School, Miss., 1 February 1971.
Keirn, Miss Nellie, Columbus, Miss., 15 March 1971.
Kolb, Mrs. C. M., Aberdeen, Miss., 6 November 1970.
Lampton, Mrs. R. B., Jackson, Miss., 13 November 1970.
Lancaster, Mrs. J. T., Sunflower, Miss., 8 January 1971.
Lott, T. E., Sr., Columbus, Miss., 15 March 1971.
Melton, Mrs. Julius W., Clinton, Miss., 12 November 1969.
McClellan, Attorney Thompson, West Point, Miss., 12 January 1971.
McElroy, Judge T. H., Oxford, Miss., 11 January 1971.
Morrow, R. D., Jackson, Miss., 1 February 1971.
Overstreet, Lee, Sr., McHenry, Miss., 20 March 1971.
Overstreet, N. W., Jackson, Miss., 17 November 1969.
Painter, Mrs. L. G., Jackson, Miss., 13 November 1970.

BIBLIOGRAPHY

Peugh, Mrs. W. G., Sr., Aberdeen, Miss., 6 November 1970.
Phillips, Mrs. W. S., Pontotoc, Miss., 12 December 1970.
Pinkinton, Mrs. Talmadge St., Artesia, Miss., 15 March 1971.
Price, D. H., Prentiss, Miss., 1 February 1971.
Price, Mrs. W. E., Clinton, Miss., 30 June 1971.
Robinson, O. N., Red Bay, Ala., 12 January 1971.
Sanders, Miss Marcie, Columbus, Miss., 3 November 1970.
Sheldon, Mrs. H. E., Westminster, S. C., 18-19 May 1971.
Smith, Arthur, Pascagoula, Miss., 20 March 1971.
Smith, John T., Jackson, Miss., 1 February 1971.
Sweat, Judge N. S., Corinth, Miss., 12 January 1970.
Taylor, Mrs. Swep S., Jackson, Miss., 13 November 1970.
Therrell, T. L., Florence, Miss., 9 April 1971.
Therrell, Mrs. T. L., Florence, Miss., 9 April 1971.
Walker, Howard, Florence, Miss., 9 April 1971.
Wall, Cowan, Meridian, Miss., 22 April 1971.
Watts, Mrs. Robert, Kosciusko, Miss., 10 December 1971.
Webster, H. D., Oxford, Miss., 11 January 1971.
Webster, Mrs. H. D., Oxford, Miss., 11 January 1971.
Welborn, Miss Winifred, Laurel, Miss., 3 February 1971.
Whitfield, Billy W., Columbus, Miss., 21 October 1970.
Whitfield, Dr. Edmund, Florence, Miss., 9 April 1971.
Whitfield, Henry M., Tupelo, Miss., 13 March 1971.
Whitfield, Dr. John S., Florence, Miss., 9 April 1971.
Whitfield, R. A., Columbus, Miss., 15 March 1971.
Whitney, Mrs. Claudia, Jackson, Miss., 13 November 1970.
Wiltsee, Herbert L., Atlanta, Ga., 29 March 1973.
Woodward, Mrs. Jones, Kosciusko, Miss., 10 December 1970.

Letters

Abel, Mrs. Mary Dunn, McComb, Miss., 1 March 1971.
Addkison, Mrs. H. M., Jackson, Miss., 13 April 1971.
Allen, Mrs. B. B., Indianola, Miss., 15 April 1971.
Anders, Mrs. Ruth R., Gautier, Miss., 13 January 1971.
Antley, Miss Annie L., Forest, Miss., 26 January 1971.
Armstrong, Miss Caro, Columbus, Miss., 16 March 1971.
Atkins, Mrs. I. H., Columbus, Miss., 9 January 1971.
Atkinson, Mrs. Eloise, Ames, Iowa, 15 January 1971.
Aust, Mrs. Olivia Tucker, Tunica, Miss., 3 February 1971.
Austin, Miss Luna, Ellisville, Miss., 28 January 1971.
Barnett, Mrs. Vera, Blue Mountain, Miss., 25 January 1971.
Barnett, Mrs. W. M., Bonaire, Ga., 28 January 1971.

Bealle, Mrs. J. B., Greenwood, Miss., 1 February 1971.
Best, Mrs. Courtney, Cleveland, Miss., 25 March 1971.
Bland, Mrs. G. B., Lorman, Miss., 1 February 1971.
Blunk, Mrs. Mayme H., Ellisville, Miss., 23 January 1971.
Bobo, Mrs. Robert E., Clarksdale, Miss., 27 January 1971.
Bolian, Mrs. Orleane P., Jackson, Miss., 12 January 1971.
Bond, Miss Alice, Charlotte, N.C., 19 January 1971.
Bond, Mrs. Irene T., Pace, Miss., 26 January 1971.
Booker, Mrs. T. E., Portland, Tenn., 20 January 1971.
Booth, Mrs. George H., Tupelo, Miss., 15 January 1971.
Box, Mrs. Thomas T., Fairfield, Ala., 10 February 1971.
Brewer, Mrs. O. C., Helena, Ark., 18 January 1971.
Brooks, Mrs. C. S., Memphis, Tenn., 20 January 1971.
Brougher, Mrs. W. E., McLean, Va., 24 January 1971.
Brumfield, Mrs. H. A., Portsmouth, Va., 30 January 1971.
Buchanan, James E., Blue Mountain, Miss., 17 August 1971.
Bunyard, Mrs. Clarence H., Clinton, Miss., 9 January 1971.
Bush, Mrs. R. H., Bryan, Tex., 13 January 1971.
Caffey, Mrs. S. H., Columbus, Miss., 6 February 1971.
Calvert, Miss Anita, West Point, Miss., 30 January 1971.
Carlson, Mrs. H. F., Pensacola, Fla., 11 January 1971.
Carlton, Mrs. L. E., Arkabutla, Miss., 16 February 1971.
Carpenter, Miss Maude, Starkville, Miss., 15 February 1971.
Carruth, Miss Alberta, Decatur, Ga., 29 January 1971.
Caulfeild, Miss Ruby, Woodville, Miss., 12 January 1971.
Chapman, Mrs. Lewis C., Fairhope, Ala., 4 February 1971.
Charles, Mrs. G. A., Texarkana, Tex., 19 January 1971.
Cheatham, Miss Catherine, Meridian, Miss., 6 February 1971.
Clark, Mrs. Charles F., Hendersonville, N.C., 29 April 1971.
Clark, Mrs. Clyde F., Silver Spring, Md., 25 January 1971.
Clark, Mrs. S. J., Sr., Fayetteville, N.C., 20 January 1971.
Clowe, Mrs. Carrie H., Jackson, Miss., 19 March 1971.
Connell, Mrs. M. L., Wartrace, Tenn., 13 January 1971.
Connor, Mrs. R. S., Houston, Tex., 16 April 1971.
Culbertson, Miss Beulah, Columbus, Miss., 1 March 1971.
Daniel, Mrs. C. E., Atlanta, Ga., 15 January 1971.
Daniel, Mrs. E. E., Birmingham, Ala., 26 February 1971.
Deen, Mrs. C. E., Hattiesburg, Miss., 29 January 1971.
Denman, Miss Annie, Jackson, Miss., 20 January 1971.
Dickins, Miss Dorothy, Greenwood, Miss., 25 January 1971.
Dietrich, Mrs. E. George, Waterloo, N.Y., 12 February 1971.
Dittman, Mrs. F. W., Memphis, Tenn., 11 January 1971.
Doane, Mrs. E. Guy, Seneca Falls, N.Y., 1 February 1971.

BIBLIOGRAPHY

Edwards, Mrs. Mattie Hammond, Troy, Tex., 2 March 1971.
Eichelberger, Dr. Marietta, Chicago, Ill., 16 January 1971.
Ellington, Mrs. Lena B., Arlington, Va., 2 March 1971.
Ernst, Mrs. Lillian Thyne, Durant, Miss., 15 June 1971.
Estopinal, Mrs. Claudia Anderson, Meridian, Miss., 19 February 1971.
Ferguson, Mrs. R. L., Jackson, Tenn., 26 January 1971.
Fleming, Mrs. E. C., Jackson, Miss., 15 February 1971.
Foil, Mrs. L. B., Bogalusa, La., 11 January 1971.
Foster, Mrs. Ray, Tchula, Miss., 5 February 1971.
Franz, Mrs. Anne H., Jacksonville, Fla., 25 January 1971.
Gaines, Mrs. C. S., Coldwater, Miss., 27 January 1971.
Galbreath, Mrs. J. M., Houston, Tex., 14 January 1971.
Gay, Mrs. W. W., St. Petersburg, Fla., 12 January 1971.
George, Mrs. A. C., Panama City, Fla., 19 January 1971.
Gibbons, Mrs. Thomas M., Laurel, Miss., 15 January 1971.
Gladney, Mr. Constance Burnett, Panama City, Fla., 13 January 1971.
Glazener, Mrs. Mabeth, Dallas, Tex., 5 February 1971.
Goza, Mrs. A. F., Rosedale, Miss., 19 January 1971.
Gunter, Mrs. R. B., Florence, Miss., 13 February 1971.
Hardy, Mrs. Miles, Tyler, Ala., 8 February 1971.
Hagerty, Mrs. H. S., Hattiesburg, Miss., 13 January 1971.
Harlan, Mrs. Wall E., Jackson, Miss., 9 February 1971.
Harmon, Francis S., New York, N.Y., 27 February 1972.
Harned, Mrs. H. H., Sr., State College, Miss., 10 January 1971.
Harrell, Mrs. William R., Decatur, Miss., 2 February 1971.
Hartness, Miss Laurie, Trenton, Ga., 30 January 1971.
Heffner, Miss Lillian, Indianola, Miss., 24 February 1971.
Helland, Mrs. Olin H., Douglas, Ga., 12 January 1971.
Hester, Miss Ruth, Jackson, Miss., 8 February 1971.
Hightower, Mrs. Charles C., Hattiesburg, Miss., 27 February 1971.
Hodge, Mrs. G. C., Ocean Springs, Miss., 23 February, 1971.
Hollingsworth, Mrs. Frank, West, Miss., 14 June 1971.
Holmes, Miss Lois, Moultrie, Ga., 27 January 1971.
Hooper, Miss Emma L., Memphis, Tenn., 18 March 1970.
Hopkins, Miss Nan, Memphis, Tenn., 13 February 1971.
Horne, Mrs. D. O., Belzoni, Miss., 3 February 1971.
Howard, Mrs. Lucy, Columbus, Miss., 12 January 1971.
Howorth, Mrs. Lucy Somerville, Cleveland, Miss., 23 February 1971.
Howell, Miss Ellen, Carthage, Miss., 1 October 1971.
Huenefeld, Mrs. Arnold, Gregory, Ark., 3 March 1971.

Humphries, Mrs. J. D., Douglas, Ga., 3 February 1971.
Jackson, Miss Willery, Hattiesburg, Miss., 1 February 1971.
Johnson, Miss Annie Lee, Lauderdale, Miss., 8 February 1971.
Johnson, Mrs. Arrington, Columbus, Miss., 6 February 1971.
Johnson, Felix M., West Point, Miss., 30 September 1969.
Johnson, Mrs. Ida K., Washington, D. C., 22 January 1971.
Johnson, Mrs. Marie D., Dayton, Ohio, 6 February 1971.
Jones, Mrs. Carmilita W., Houston, Tex., 1 February 1971.
Jones, Mrs. L. I., Grenada, Miss., 4 February 1971.
Kelly, Mrs. R. Ellis, Kosciusko, Miss., 14 January 1971.
Kendrick, F. A., Water Valley, Miss., 13 March 1971.
Kethley, Mr. William Marion, Cleveland, Miss., 21 October 1971.
Kroll, Mrs. William E., Carlisle, Penn., 13 January 1971.
Land, Fred H., Greenville, S.C., 13 April 1971.
Lawler, Miss Nell, Cleveland, Miss., 29 January 1971.
Ledwith, Mrs. W. M., Daytona Beach, Fla., 13 January 1971.
Lee, Mrs. H. Sam, Jr., McComb, Miss., 29 January 1971.
Leech, Mrs. K. D., Sr., Smithville, Miss., 7 February 1971.
Lester, Mrs. Dozier, Inverness, Miss., 22 January 1971.
Levy, Mrs. Undine, Memphis, Tenn., 23 January 1971.
Lewis, Mrs. Roy, Columbus, Miss., 28 January 1971.
Lindley, Mrs. Bertrand H., Vicksburg, Miss., 8 February 1971.
Llewellyn, Mrs. L. B., Baldwyn, Miss., 15 January 1971.
Long, Sam H., Tupelo, Miss., 22 February 1971.
Loper, Mrs. Ruth D., Meridian, Miss., 9 February 1971.
Lott, Edwin, New Orleans, La., 5 May 1971.
Lowe, Mrs. M. E., Glendora, Miss., 24 April 1971.
Lusk, Mrs. S. T., Oxford, Miss., 28 January, 1971.
Lutken, Mrs. Peter K., Jackson, Miss., 13 January 1971.
Mabus, Mrs. R. E., Ackerman, Miss., 13 January 1971.
Marable, Mrs. W. E., Jr., Memphis, Tenn., 27 January 1971.
Martin, Mrs. Elizabeth Stubbs, Greenwood, Miss., 2 February 1971.
Massengale, Dr. Grace, Hattiesburg, Miss., 13 January 1971.
Mattingly, Dr. Marie Dees, New Orleans, La., 11 February 1971.
McCain, Mrs. Connie, Houston, Miss., 11 January 1971.
McClanahan, Mrs. W. H., Columbus, Miss., 20 January 1971.
McCulloch, Mrs. M. F., Grenada, Miss., 19 February 1971.
McCullough, Mrs. Boyce, Memphis, Tenn., 30 January 1971.
McDuffie, Mrs. William R., Warrington, Fla., 21 January 1971.
McEwen, Mrs. C. R., Paducah, Ky., 13 March 1971.
McIntyre, Mrs. Viola Burns, Brandon, Miss., 15 January 1971.
McIntyre, W. E., Esq., Brandon, Miss., 15 January 1971.
McKee, Mrs. Fred, Washington, D. C., 25 January 1971.

BIBLIOGRAPHY

McLean, Mrs. D. C., Memphis, Tenn., 18 January 1971.
McLean, Mrs. J. L., Greenwood, Miss., 11 January 1971.
McNair, Mrs. K. R., Brookhaven, Miss., 15 January 1971.
Meacham, Mrs. Bera James, Hopkinsville, Ky., 11 January 1971.
Merrill, Mrs. Bergen Stelle, Olive Branch, Miss., 10 January 1971.
Middleton, Mrs. Rufus E., Brookhaven, Miss., 20 February 1971.
Mitchell, Mrs. R. S., Starkville, Miss., 3 March 1971.
Moore, Miss Maniza, Coldwater, Miss., 23 January 1971.
Mulloy, Mrs. R. E., Laurel, Miss., 11 January 1971.
Nelson, Mrs. R. M., Crystal Springs, Miss., 3 February 1971.
Newman, Mrs. Virginia M., Memphis, Tenn., 22 May 1971.
Oliver, Mrs. W. C., Monroe, La., 30 January 1971.
Oswalt, Mrs. Z. E., Washington, Miss., 12 February 1971.
Page, Mrs. M. E., Memphis, Tenn., 29 January 1971.
Palmer, Mrs. Wilmot H., Ruleville, Miss., 20 January 1971.
Parish, Mrs. Janie G., Samson, Ala., 18 February 1971.
Parker, Mrs. Charles G., St. Petersburg, Fla., 9 February 1971.
Patty, Mrs. E. L., Tupelo, Miss., 11 January 1971.
Pelt, Mrs. Clinton Van, Sellersburg, Ind., 26 January 1971.
Perkins, Mrs. J. D., Grand Junction, Colo., 25 January 1971.
Phillips, Mrs. Adam, Knoxville, Tenn., 17 February 1971.
Phillips, Mrs. E. L., Columbus, Miss., 13 February 1971.
Pollard, Mrs. Clarence O., Hemet, Ca., 30 January 1971.
Pollard, Mrs. R. V., Greenwood, Miss., 12 January 1971.
Pope, Mrs. James D., Cocoa Beach, Fla., 27 February 1971.
Pope, Mrs. W. E., Ocean Springs, Miss., 21 January 1971.
Posey, Baker F., New Orleans, La., 3 May 1971.
Powell, Mrs. Charles H., Powder Springs, Ga., 8 February 1971.
Powers, Mrs. Robert S., Dallas, Tex., 1 February 1971.
Pylant, Miss Yuba, Purvis, Miss., 28 January 1971.
Quick, C. Hooker, Picayune, Miss., 21 December 1970.
Ragland, Mrs. C. H., Starkville, Miss., 31 January 1971.
Ranck, Mrs. William A., Baltimore, Md., 27 January 1971.
Redden, Mrs. W. S., Pace, Miss., 27 January 1971.
Reed, Mrs. L. Blance, Moultrie, Ga., 31 January 1971.
Reeves, Mrs. Bert, Tuscaloosa, Ala., 11 January 1971.
Rigler, Mrs. C. P., Philadelphia, Miss., 11 January 1971.
Riley, Dr. Martin L., Jackson, Miss., 25 April 1971.
Ross, Mrs. J. E., Greenwood, Miss., 12 January 1971.
Rowan, Mrs. Dudley, Amory, Miss., 2 February 1971.
Rowzee, Mrs. Gertrude, Jackson, Miss., 16 January 1971.
Russell, Mrs. R. H., South Hadley, Mass., 12 January 1971.
Safley, Mrs. J. A., Rome, Miss., 13 January 1971.

Sayle, Mrs. Elizabeth J., Oakland, Miss., 17 January 1971.
Simmons, Mrs. Elizabeth E., Columbus, Miss., 9 January 1971.
Shands, Mrs. Alma W., Jackson, Miss., 2 February 1971.
Shields, Mrs. T. H., Greenville, Mississippi, 19 January 1971.
Shipman, Mrs. W. Carl, Hendersonville, N.C., 15 February 1971.
Slay, Mrs. Carlton L., Toledo, Ohio, 7 February 1971.
Smith, Mrs. Claude R., Holly Springs, Miss., 27 January 1971.
Smith, Mrs. Clyde, Prentiss, Miss., 13 January 1971.
Smith, Mrs. Harry L., Jackson, Miss., 7 October 1971.
Smith, Miss Mary, Indianola, Miss., 26 January 1971.
Smith, Mrs. O. Z., Lucedale, Miss., 31 January 1971.
Snider, Mrs. J. B., Pascagoula, Miss., 11 January 1971.
Soubier, Mrs. H. C., Evanston, Ill., 26 January 1971.
Spurlock, Mrs. K. L., Columbus, Miss., 10 January 1971.
Steele, Mrs. X. O., Brookhaven, Miss., 22 January 1971.
Stephens, Mrs. C. R., Brooksville, Fla., 13 January 1971.
Stokes, Mrs. Alwin, Winnfield, La., 11 March 1971.
Street, Miss Lottie, Fort Worth, Tex., 19 January 1971.
Swor, Dr. Chester, Jackson, Miss., 18 December 1970.
Taylor, Mrs. William Sledge, Sledge, Miss., 10 January 1971.
Therrell, Mrs. J. S., Macon, Miss., 11 January 1971.
Thomas, Mrs. Mamie, Senatobia, Miss., 11 January 1971.
Turner, Mrs. W. L., Bourbon, Miss., 23 February 1971.
Vaughan, Mrs. Fay, Ridgeland, Miss., 3 February 1971.
Veazey, Mrs. Thurmond, Senatobia, Miss., 2 February 1971.
Vickers, Miss Dovie, Hammond, La., 11 February 1971.
Vincent, Mrs. Fannie N., Forest, Miss., 26 January 1971.
Wadlington, Mrs. Mernice T., Biloxi, Miss., 26 January 1971.
Wallace, Mrs. J. W., Edinburg, Tex., 17 January 1971.
Walters, Mrs. T. Jeff, Ellisville, Miss., 14 January 1971.
Waring, Mrs. A. L., Hughes, Ark., 15 January 1971.
Watson, Miss Ada, Columbus, Miss., 7 February 1971.
Weaver, Miss Bessie, Columbus, Miss., 9 January 1971.
Webb, Miss Allie M., Hattiesburg, Miss., 10 February 1971.
West, Mrs. E. C., Columbus, Miss., 23 February 1971.
Wheat, Mrs. W. E., Pensacola, Fla., 13 January 1971.
White, Miss Laura, Biloxi, Miss., 21 October 1969.
White, Mrs. Morris Edward, Tampa, Fla., 15 January 1971.
Whitfield, Miss Alice M., Demopolis, Ala., 25 January 1971.
Whitfield, Miss Nelly K., Montgomery, Ala., 28 January 1971.
Wichman, Fred, Chattanooga, Tenn., 26 April 1971.
Willis, Mrs. P. H., Grenada, Miss., 9 January 1971.
Wiggins, Mrs. Winifred Y., Rocky Mount, N.C., 20 February 1971.

164 BIBLIOGRAPHY

Wigransky, Mrs. Lillian Pace, Lake, Miss., 19 January 1971.
Wilkinson, Mrs. R. E., Heidelberg, Miss., 25 January 1971.
Wingate, Mrs. Annie Campbell, Greenville, Miss., 10 January 1971.
Wood, Mrs. E. Watson, Ocean Springs, Miss., 24 March 1971.
Woodward, Mrs. Shelby, Louisville, Miss., 4 February 1971.
Woolfolk, Mrs. John, Atlanta, Ga., 15 January 1971.
Young, Mrs. S. C., Canton, Miss., 22 January 1971.

E. LEGAL DOCUMENTS, BULLETINS, AND REPORTS

Biennial Report of the Adjutant General of the State of Mississippi (1927).
Biennial Report of the Auditor Public Accounts of the State of Mississippi (1927).
Biennial Report of the Board of Trustees, Superintendent and Other of the Mississippi State Penitentiary (1927).
Biennial Report of the Mississippi Department of Agriculture and Commerce (1928).
Biennial Report of the Mississippi School for the Deaf (1927).
Biennial Report of the Mississippi State Forestry Commission (1927).
Biennial Report of the Mississippi State Insane Hospital (1927).
Biennial Report of the Mississippi State Superintendent of Public Education (1899, 1901, 1903, 1905, 1907, 1909).
Biennial Report of the Secretary of State—for Mississippi (1923, 1925, 1927, 1929, 1931).
Biennial Report of the State Board of Health of the State of Mississippi (1925).
Biennial Report of the State Highway Commission—for Mississippi (1927).
Biennial Report of the State Treasurer of the State of Mississippi (1927).
Biennial Report of the State Vocational Board on Vocational Education (1925).
Bulletin of the Mississippi Industrial Institute and College (1908-1909, March 1910, June 1912, June 1913, May 1914, June 1914, June 1918, June 1919).
Financial Report of the Mississippi Industrial Institute and College (1909-1911, 1911-1913).
Mississippi *House Journal* (1924, 1926).
Mississippi *Laws* (1900, 1902, 1904, 1908, 1920, 1924, 1926).
Mississippi *Senate Journal* (1926).
Report of President Whitfield to the Board of Trustees of the

BIBLIOGRAPHY 165

Higher Educational Institutions of Mississippi (July 1917, a copy of original; 1919).
School Laws of Mississippi (1900).
Statistical Abstract of the United States, 1909, 1911, 1923. Washington, D.C., 1910, 1912, 1923 respectively.
Thirteenth Census of the United States. Washington, D.C., 1913.

F. NEWSPAPERS

Aberdeen Weekly (1878–1933).
Bay St. Louis Sea Coast Echo (1892–).
Belzoni Banner (1906–).
Brandon News (1892–).
Canton Madison County Herald (1906–).
Clarksdale Daily Register (1908–).
Columbia Marion County Progress (1909–1935).
Columbus Commercial (1893–1922).
Columbus Commercial Dispatch (1922–).
Columbus Mississippi State College for Women Spectator (1903–).
Greenville Daily Democrat-Times (1917–1938).
Grenada Sentinel (1854–1955).
Holly Springs South Reporter (1920–).
Houston Times Post (1913–).
Jackson Baptist Record (1877–).
Jackson Daily Clarion-Ledger (1888–).
Jackson Daily News (1907–).
Jackson Evening News (1892–1907).
Jackson Mississippi Free Lance (1923–1928).
Jackson Vardaman's Weekly (1908–1923).
Jackson Woman Voter (1921–1923).
McComb Enterprise (1889–1945).
Memphis Commercial Appeal (1840–).
Memphis News Scimitar (n. d.).
Memphis Press Scimitar (1880–).
Meridian Star (1893–).
New York Times (1851–).
Pascagoula Chronicle Star (1858–1966).
Pontotoc Sentinel (1894–1930).
Poplarville Free Press (1890–1939).
Raleigh Smith County Reformer (1892–).
Raymond Hinds County Reformer (n. d.).
Ripley Southern Sentinel (1879–).
State College Mississippi State University Reflector (1888–).

166 BIBLIOGRAPHY

Vicksburg *Herald* (1859–1957).
West Point *Leader* (1892–1928).
Winona *Times* (1884–   ).
Yazoo City *Herald* (1874–   ).
Yazoo City County *News* (1901–1932).
Yazoo City *Sentinel* (1876–1946).

II. SECONDARY WORKS

A. BOOKS

Bettersworth, John K. *Mississippi Yesterday and Today.* Austin: Steck-Vaughn, 1964.
Bond, Willard, F. *I Had A Friend.* Kansas City: E. L. Menden Hall, Inc., 1958.
Butts, R. Freeman, and Cremin, Lawrence A. *A History of Education in American Culture.* New York: Holt, Rinehart and Winston, 1953.
Chalmers, David M. *Hooded Americanism: The First Century of the Ku Klux Klan 1865–1965.* New York: Doubleday, 1969.
Clymer, Floyd. *Treasury of Early American Automobiles.* New York: McGraw-Hill, 1950.
Corlew, Robert E.; Folmsbee, Stanley J.; and Mitchell, Enoch L. *Tennessee, A Short History.* Knoxville: University of Tennessee Press, 1969.
Dabney, Charles William. *Universal Education in the South.* 2 vols. Chapel Hill: University of North Carolina Press, 1956.
Friend, A. B. *Mississippi's Senior United States Senator.* 1946.
Goodsell, Willystine. "The Education of Women," *Twenty-five Years of American Education.* Edited by I. L. Kandel. New York: Macmillan, 1969.
Grantham, Dewey W., Jr. *Hoke Smith and the Politics of the New South.* Baton Rouge: Louisiana State University Press, 1958.
──────. *The Democratic South.* Athens: University of Georgia Press, 1963.
Green, A. Wigfall. *The Man Bilbo.* Baton Rouge: Louisiana State University Press, 1963.
Guyton, Pearl Vivian. *The History of Mississippi.* New York: Iroquois, 1935.
Hickman, Nollie. *Mississippi Harvest: Lumbering in the Longleaf Pine Belt 1840–1915.* University, Miss.: The University of Miss., 1962.

History of the First Baptist Church, Columbus, Mississippi, 1832–1964. Columbus, 1964.
Holmes, William F. *The White Chief, James Kimble Vardaman.* Baton Rouge: Louisiana State University Press, 1970.
Key, V. O., Jr. *Southern Politics in State and Nation.* New York: Vintage Books, 1949.
Kirby, Jack Temple. *Westmoreland Davis, Virginia Planter-Politician, 1859–1942.* Charlottesville: University Press of Virginia, 1968.
Kirwan, Albert D. *Revolt of the Rednecks: Mississippi Politics, 1876–1925.* Lexington: University of Kentucky Press, 1951.
Knight, Edgar W. *Public Education in the South.* Boston: Ginn & Co., 1922.
Luthin, Reinhard H. *American Demagogues Twentieth Century.* Gloucester: Beacon Press, 1959.
McLemore, Richard Aubrey, ed. *A History of Mississippi.* 2 vols. Hattiesburg: University and College Press of Mississippi, 1973.
Mitchell, Broadus, and Mitchell, George Sinclair. *The Industrial Revolution in the South.* Baltimore: Johns Hopkins Press, 1930.
Mississippi State Hospital. *Centennial Program.* 1955.
Monroe, Paul. *A Text-Book in the History of Education.* New York: Macmillan Co., 1906.
Moore, Albert Burton. *History of Alabama.* Tuscaloosa: Alabama Book Store, 1934.
Moore, John Robert. *Senator Josiah William Bailey of North Carolina.* Durham: Duke University Press, 1968.
Nixon, Raymond B. *Henry W. Grady: Spokesman of the New South.* New York: Alfred A. Knopf, 1943.
Noble, Stuart Grayson. *Forty Years of the Public Schools in Mississippi.* New York: Teachers College, Columbia University, 1918.
O'Shea, M. V. *A State Educational System At Work.* Jackson: B. B. Jones Fund, 1927.
Proctor, Samuel. *Napoleon Bonaparte Broward, Florida's Fighting Democrat.* Gainesville: University of Florida Press, 1950.
Rhodes, M. C. *History of Taxation in Mississippi, 1798–1929.* Nashville George Peabody College for Teachers, 1930.
Rowland, Dunbar. *History of Mississippi: The Heart of the South.* 4 vols. Jackson: S. J. Clarke Publishing Company, 1925.
_____. *The Official and Statistical Register of the State of Mississippi 1924–1928.* New York: J. J. Little and Ives Co., 1928.
Saloutos, Theodore. *Farmer Movements in the South 1865–1933.* Berkeley: University of California Press, 1960.
Sanders, Marcie D. *The Pohl of Memories.* 1967.

BIBLIOGRAPHY

Simkins, Francis B. *A History of the South.* New York: Knopf, 1963.
Sydnor, Charles S., and Bennett, Claude. *Mississippi History.* New York: Rand, McNally & Co., 1930.
Taylor, Walter Nesbit, and Ethridge, George H. *Mississippi: A History.* 4 vols. Hopkinsville: The Historical Record Association, 1940.
Thwing, Charles Franklin. *A History of Education in the United States Since the Civil War.* Boston: Houghton Mifflin Co., 1910.
Tindall, George Brown. *The Emergence of the New South, 1913-1945.* A History of the South, edited by Wendell Holmes Stephenson and E. Merton Coulter, vol. 10. Baton Rouge: Louisiana State University Press, 1967.
Underwood, Felix J., and Whitfield, R. N. *Public Health and Medical Licensure in the State of Mississippi, 1718-1937.* Jackson: Tucker Printing House, 1938.
Watson, A. J., Jr. *Electric Power and People Power: The Story of the Mississippi Power Company.* New York New York Newcomen Society, 1969.
Whitfield, Theodore Marshall, ed. *Whitfield, Bryan, Smith, and Related Families* n. p., n. d., owned by Billy W. Whitfield, Columbus, Mississippi.
Williams, T. Harry. *Huey Long.* New York: Knopf, 1969.
Wilson, Charles H. *Education For Negroes in Mississippi Since 1910.* Boston: Meador Publishing Co., 1947.
Wish, Harvey. *Society and Thought in Modern America.* 2 vols. New York: D. McKay Co., 1952.
Woodward, C. Vann. *Origins of the New South, 1877-1913.* A History of the South, edited by Wendell Holmes Stephenson and E. Merton Coulter, vol. 9. Baton Rouge: Louisiana State University Press, 1951.

B. PERIODICALS

Cason, Clarence E. "The Mississippi Imbroglio." *Virginia Quarterly Review* 7(1931):229-40.
Editorial. *The Mississippi Educational Advance* 10(1919):10-11.
Editorial. *The Mississippi Educational Advance* 3(1914):2.
Editorial. *The Mississippi School Journal* 7(1902):642.
Fant, Anne L. "Henry Lewis Whitfield, Educator, Governor, Christian Gentleman." *The Mississippi Educational Advance* 18(1927): 313-14.
Hataway, Marsha Perry. "The Development of the Mississippi State

Highway System, 1916–1932." *The Journal of Mississippi History* 28(1966):286–303.

"I. I. & C. Notes." *The Mississippi Educational Advance* 7(1918):18.

Kethley, William Marion. "A Brief History of Delta State College." *The Journal of Mississippi History* 19(1957):173–84.

Leavell, Reverend Roland Q. "Memorial To Governor Whitfield." *The Church Chimes*. 20 March 1927.

McCain, William D. "The Life and Labor of Dennis Murphree." *The Journal of Mississippi History* 12(1962):183-91.

———. "Theodore Gilmore Bilbo and the Mississippi Delta." *The Journal of Mississippi History* 12(1969):1–27.

Mississippi Industrial Institute and College. *Meh Lady* 7(1908).

Mississippi State College for Women Alumnae News Bulletin (Spring 1971).

"Notes From the Colleges." *The Mississippi School Journal* 13(1909):21.

O'Shea, M. V. "A Modern Pestalozzi." *The Wisconsin Journal of Education* 43(1911):92

Rice, Nannie H. "Mississippi." *The American Mercury* 7(1926): 77-82.

Scott, Anne Firor. "After Suffrage: Southern Women in the Twenties." *The Journal of Southern History* 30(1964):298–318.

"South Wide Conference Termed Great Success." *The Mississippi Developer* 1(1925):2.

Walton, Lester A. "Whitfield—Apostle of Racial Good Will." *New Outlook* 136(1924):589–91.

"Why Mississippi Chose A Demagogue." *The Outlook* 147(1927): 3–4.

C. DISSERTATIONS AND THESES

Balsamo, Larry Thomas. "Theodore G. Bilbo and Mississippi Politics, 1877–1932." Ph.D. dissertation, University of Missouri, 1967.

Eason, Thomas Rogers. "An Analysis of Historical Factors in Mississippi's Economic Development With Implications for Future Growth." Ph.D. dissertation, University of Mississippi, 1968.

James, Thomas Garner. "A History of the Mississippi Gulf Coast From November 11, 1919 to November 11, 1928." M.A. thesis, University of Mississippi, 1935.

Massey, Edwin Bernard. "Development of the Anti-Evolution Bill in the Mississippi Legislature in 1926." M.A. thesis, University of Mississippi, 1966.

Mosley, Donald C. "A History of Labor Unions in Mississippi." Ph.D. dissertation, University of Alabama, 1965.

Humphrey, George Duke. "Public Education for Whites in Mississippi." Ph.D. dissertation, Ohio State University, 1939.

Ratliff, Sarah Frances: "The Career of Thomas Lowry Bailey." M.A. thesis, Mississippi State University, 1952.

Stewart, Dallas. "Development of Public Health in Mississippi." M.A. thesis, University of Mississippi, 1932.

INDEX

Agricultural High Schools, 25–26
Atwell, ETTA, 71, 79–80
Bailey, Thomas, 118
BAWI Program, 130
Bell, Jeff, 97
Bell, Percy, 80, 92
Bilbo, Theodore G., 80, 82, 84, 86, 87, 90, 92, 94, 96–97
Birkhead, Frances, 80, 96
Bolivar County Agricultural High School, 75
Bonser, F. G., 72
Boswell, Henry, 101
Boyd, G. G., 35
Brawley, F. M., 72
Brewer, Earl, 71, 92
Broward, Napoleon B., 132
Bryan, Harry, 92
Conference for Education in the South, 20
Cook, Joe, 81
Curry, J. L. M., 13
Dabney, Robert L., 15
Davis, Westmoreland, 142
Delta State University, 137
Dinkins, Macey, 101
Eastland, James O., 84
Education: description of and development in the South, 1876–1900, 14–22; vocational training, 25; agricultural high schools, 25–26; physical education, 26; normal schools, 32–33; illiteracy, 1900–1910, 37. *See also* Conference for Education in the South; Southern Education Board; General Education Board; Smith-Hughes Act
Ewing, T. G., 109

Farmer's Alliance, 19
Farmer's Credit Association, 135
Fitzhugh, Mollie, 5
Fox, T. L., 143
Franklin, Lester, 80
Franklin, T. B., 71
Franks, Rev. J. D., 149
General Education Board, 20
George, James Z., 93
George, Joe, 118
Grady, Henry W., 130
Grange, 91
Grantham, Dewey, 118
Hewitt, Purser, 101
Hewitt, Rev. W. A., 100, 148–149
High School Textbook Commission, 138
Hull, William, 75
Hume, Alfred, 92
Inman, Cecil, 119, 120, 123, 125
Ivy, H. M., 24
Jones, Bernard B., 69, 75
Jones, Lawrence C., 13
Keirn, Nellie, 71
Kennedy, Lawrence, 118
Kethley, Mrs. William M., 137
Kincannon, A. A., 9, 40
Ku Klux Klan, 107–108
Lamar, L. Q. C., 93
Lawrence, O. F., 71
Lee County Fair, 91
Long, Sam, 108
Lott, T. E., Sr., 65
Lowndes County Farm Bureau, 68
McLaurin, A. J., 9, 38, 92
McLaurin, Sydney, 92
Mann, Horace, 22
Mississippi A&M College, 25

172 Index

Mississippi Day, 27
Mississippi Normal College, 33
Mississippi University for Women: Mable Ward Practice House, 47; Shattuck Hall, 47; Zouave Drill, 50.
Mississippi School Journal, 37
Mississippi State Library Commission, 138
Mississippi State University, 25
Mitchell, C. D., 133
Model Farm, 69
Mooney, C. P. J., 58
Morrison, Cameron, 140
Morrow, R. D., 145
Murphree, Dennis, 100, 117, 118, 119, 123
Negro, 107-111
Neilson, Sarah, 50
Neshoba County Fair, 91
Newspapers: influence of in 1923 gubernatorial campaign, 92-93
Normal schools, 32-33
O'Shea, M. V., 72
Overstreet, N. W., 132
Parker, John M., 123
Patron's Union, 91
Peay, Austin, 138
Physical Education, 26
Piney Woods School, 13
Pohl, Emma Ody, 49-50
Populist Party, 19
Provine, J. W., 92
Rand, Clayton, 150
Rice, Nannie, 135
Roosevelt, Theodore, 151
Russell, Lee, 80, 96, 99-100, 101
Sale, Frances, 69
Scales, Erie C., 100
Seaman, John E., 14
Sillers, Walter, 118
Smith, Hoke, 142
Smith, Sydney M., 100
Smith-Hughes Act, 23
Southern Education Board, 20-21
Southern Governor's Conference, 112
Stephens, H. D., 92
S. T. Payer letter, 69-70
Sunday, Rev. Billy, 106
Sweat, N. S., 139
Taft, William Howard, 58

Taylor, Mrs. Swep S., 89
Thorndike, E. L., 23
Tindall, George B., 118
Underwood, Felix J., 134
Union Labor Party, 19
University of Southern Mississippi, 137. *See also* Mississippi Normal College
Vardaman, James K., 40, 94, 97, 101, 126
Vocational Training, 25
Watson, A. J., 126
Webster, H. D., 84
Welborn, Winifred, 30
White, Hugh, 130
White, Mary Dampeer, 8
White, William, 8
Whitfield, George William, 4
Whitfield, Henry L.: birth of, 4; college experiences of, 6, 9; as school teacher, 7; marriage to Mary Dampeer White, 8; religion of, 8-9, 13, 26-27, 45, 59-60, 65, 67, 76, 106-107; receives appointment as Mississippi State Superintendent of Education, 9; and philosophy of education, 10-13; accomplishments as State Superintendent of Education, 25-28, 30, 32-37; authorizes building of miniature plant at Mississippi A&M College, 25; and agricultural high schools, 25-26; encourages physical education, 26; accents patriotism, 27; on home life, 28-29; improves teacher training, 30, 32-33; on normal schools, 32-33; corrects weaknesses in rural schools, 34; and library movement, 35; establishes journal, 36-37; improves literacy, 37; becomes president of Mississippi Industrial Institute and College, 40; on philosophy of higher education, 40-47; accomplishments as president of Mississippi Industrial Institute and College, 47-52, 54-60; improves college grounds, 47; authorizes construction of Shattuck Hall and Mable Ward Practice House, 47; reorganizes Normal Department, 47-49; on home economics, 51; on agriculture and

floriculture, 51–52; strengthens faculty, 54–55; on enrollment, 55–56; introduces student government, 57; on chapel exercises, 58–60; relationship with students, 60–64; physical appearance of, 64–65; description of Mrs. Whitfield, 65; on family life, 65; sense of humor of, 65–67; civic interests of, 67–68; becomes first president of Lowndes County Farm Bureau, 68; relationship to B. B. Jones, 69, 75; dismissed as president of Mississippi Industrial Institute and College, 73–75; announcement of candidacy for governor, 78–79; and personalities in 1923 campaign, 80; platform of, 80–82; victory statement of, 98; inaugurated governor, 99; on promotion of education, 102–105; on Know Mississippi campaign, 105; on Buy in Mississippi campaign, 105; creates opportunities in Mississippi, 105–106; attitude toward Negro, 107–111; on Wisconsin trip, 111; and Southwide Conference, 111–112; and Cotton Conference, 113; on recreation, 114; on revenue and finance, 119–125; legislative program of, 119–145; encourages industry, 125–131; establishes Mississippi State Hospital, 131–133; on agriculture, 134–135; and Mississippi Rural Credit Acts, 135; creates Mississippi State Forestry Commission, 135–136; and education in Mississippi, 136–38; on highways, 138–140; views on state penitentiary farm, 140–143; advocates law enforcement, 143; and eleemosynary institutions, 145; and veterans, 145; sickness of, 146–147; death of, 148

Whitfield, Nathan B., 4
Whitfield, Robert A., 5, 6, 38
Whitfield, R. N., 134
Williams, Rev. Howard, 106
Williams, John Sharp, 92
Williams, T. Harry, 118
Women: role in 1923 gubernatorial campaign, 86–92
Young Men's Democracy, 19